'EARTH A̶̶̶̶̶'

THE PAST, PRESENT AND FUTURE OF OUR PLANET

EXTENDED ABSTRACTS

Editors

R.T.J. Moody

R. Stoneley

C. Oldershaw

J. Larwood

2000

Published by

The Geologists' Association
LONDON

THE GEOLOGISTS' ASSOCIATION

The Geologists' Association, founded in 1858, exists to foster the progress and diffusion of the science of Geology. It holds lecture meetings in London and, via Local Groups, throughout England and Wales. It conducts field meetings and publishes Proceedings, Field Guides and Circulars regularly. For further information apply to the Honorary General Secretary, Geologists' Association, Burlington House, Piccadilly, London WIV 9AG.

All rights reserved. No part of this publication may be reproduced, stored in a retrieval system or transmitted, in any form or by any means, without the prior permission in writing of the author and the Geologists' Association.

Acknowledgments. The Geologists' Association and the Editors wish to thank Susan Brown and Susanna van Rose for their help with the manuscript and James O'Gorman and David Taylor of PDP Ltd for their skills and expertise concerned with the compilation and preparation of the text layout and overall formatting. Final thanks are due to the authors and the many sponsors of the 'Earth Alert' Festival of Geology, held in Brighton in May 2000. A list of sponsors and supporting groups is presented as the final page of this publication.

Registered Charity No. 233199

'EARTH ALERT' THE PAST, PRESENT AND FUTURE OF OUR PLANET
First Published 2000

The Geologists' Association, Burlington House, Piccadilly London W1V 9AG.
(Orders: Tel: **020 7434 9298**. Fax: **020 7207 0820**)

ISBN 0 900717 69 6

EAN 9 780900 717 691

Compiled and page set by Professional Digital Printing Ltd
21 Victoria Road, Surbiton, Surrey KT6 4JZ

Printed by Antony Rowe Limited
Bumper's Farm, Chippenham, Wiltshire SN14 6LH

Foreword

The sustainable management of our environment and its resources is among the greatest challenges facing modern society. To achieve this, understanding the diversity and dynamism of our environment, past, present and future, is essential. Our Earth heritage is at the core of this challenge.

Our Earth heritage of rocks, fossils and minerals offer us our most tangible link with an ever changing past environment. A record of species extinction and evolution, of natural disaster on a global scale, of fluctuating climates, changing environments and the rise and fall of sea level are all held within our Earth heritage. We live in an environment no less dynamic. Not only do we face the same natural changes of our geological past but, as if this was not enough, we have added our own challenging change; the human use and exploitation of natural resources.

Today our Earth heritage underpins the diversity and functioning of our environment. It directly determines soil and landscape and influences habitat and wildlife distribution. The processes which have shaped these landscapes are active now. The use and exploitation of our mineral resources has influenced every aspect of our lives.

Understanding our past allows us to predict the future. Climates have changed and will continue to change. Sea levels will continue to rise and fall. Natural disaster will happen and species will come and go. Our Earth heritage offers a direct insight into how these changes have happened, and their impact on our environment. This will allow us to better establish policy and practice for managing the future of our environment, isolating, reducing and eliminating non-sustainable human impacts on our environment and understanding and managing the impacts of natural change.

Earth Alert raises the torch for geology. The challenge now is to keep that torch alight, to lead the way into a future that is truly sustainable for our environment.

Baroness Barbara Young

Chairman
English Nature

Contents

	Page
Richard Moody. 'Earth Alert' An Introduction	1
Robert F. Symes. The Mineral World	3
John Dewey. Geology. in the 20th Century	13
Monica M. Grady. The Early Earth	15
Marian Holness. Fluids and the evolution of the Earth	21
Jane Plant. Minerals and the Natural Environment - The foundation of wealth	27
Nicholas Butterfield. Preludes to the Phanerozoic: major transitions in the early evolution of life on Earth	35
Richard Fortey. Trilobites:the world through crystal eyes.	39
Dianne Edwards. The Green Revolution	43
Mike Benton. Great Extinctions	45
Hugh Torrens. Winners and Losers – What can we learn of the future of Geology from its Past?	53
Dorrik Stow. The Ocean Planet – Excitement and Challenge of a New Frontier	59
Bill McGuire. Living on Borrowed Time - Catastrophes to Come	71
Hazel Rymer. Living with volcanic risk	77
John Mather. Groundwater Resources - Continuing Pressure on a Major Natural Resource	87
John Knill. Can the Earth safely contain our dangerous wastes?	93
Jeremy Joseph. Geology and Waste - Fluids in the environment	97
Nigel Bell. Air Pollution - The Ever-Changing Threat	105
Peter Fookes. The Construction Industry - Building on the Past	113
Richard Hardman. The Oil Industry and the Whipping Boy for a World out of Control	121
Malcolm Brown. Evolution of the Oil Industry - Its importance to the role of the Petroleum Geologist	125
Cameron Davies. Coal Mine Methane - A Fuel for the Future	129
William Fyfe. "Needed-New Earth Resource Technologies, New Geo-ethics for the 21st Century"	133
Colin Prosser & **Jonathan Larwood**. Conserving the Past to change the Future	137
David Norman. Dinosaur Research 160 Years of progress?	143

'EARTH ALERT'

Richard Moody FGS
President Geologists' Association 1998-2000

1. Introduction

The abstracts included in this book detail our knowledge of the history of planet Earth at this moment in time. Time, as we all know, passes quickly and we should remember that aged 4.55 billion years, Earth is undergoing a mid-life crisis. This has been induced by the rise and continued rise, of the most successful species ever known - humankind or Homo Sapiens. Farmers everywhere continuously deprive other species of hitherto specified niches, fishermen empty the oceans of a once bountiful harvest and industries pollute the atmosphere. The burgeoning boom in the world's population; holes in the ozone layer and widespread pollution should cause alarm bells to ring everywhere. Inept politicians, corruption and a 'live for the moment' attitude prevails however, and a crisis looms. What lessons exist in the past that can be introduced now to secure the future? Are the measures being developed today those, which will help man survive and prosper? 'Earth Alert' may point the way.

Geological history shows us that there have been dominant life forms in earlier times, it also reveals that extinction is par for the course. Remember the trilobites, ammonites, dinosaurs and more recently Neanderthal man. All gone, victims of change or competition. Will humankind go the same way?

Being brought up and educated in times defined now as politically incorrect, I was assured that man was a thinker, an innovative species, with woman being the by-product of a spare rib. Now we know that the creativity of humankind has few limitations; neither does their cruelty or their ability to exploit both their own and other species. The gentler sex may hold the answers.

No doubt, competition and adaptation were the major driving forces behind evolution during the Proterozoic (2500-550my). Competition was certainly evident throughout the Phanerozoic with 'the survival of the fittest' prevailing on a global scale. Since 'Lucy' and her relatives walked upright on the plains of Africa 4 million years ago, times have changed, the balance of power has been snatched from Mother Nature.

Initially the hominids co-existed with other species. They were hunter-gatherers, similar to the aboriginal tribes of Africa and Australasia. The ability to travel and the power to think and communicate changed this delicate relationship for ever. Innovative ideas could be passed quickly by word of mouth, dreamtime became a way of memorising tribal histories. Lessons were learned, new generations educated and gradually humankind began to control rather than respect the global environment and coeval species. We are the masters now, are we doing a good job or are we incapable of securing the future for generations to come?

Our knowledge of the past provides us with numerous thumbnail sketches of a seemingly more idyllic planet, including the sun-drenched beaches of the Jurassic and the grassy plains of the Miocene. However, sea level changes, global warming, meteorite impacts, violent earthquakes and great outpourings of basaltic lava over the Deccan denote a more turbulent past. At the present the violent storms linked to El Nino, the earthquakes of Kobe and Afghanistan and the eruptions of Mount St. Helens remind us of the powerful forces that drive both surface and sub-surface processes. Somewhere, everyday, men, women and children fall foul of such dramatic events. Strangely the more insidious but less newsworthy changes to the environment or the development of a new plague may ultimately play a more significant role in our future.

The evolution of humankind from stone-thrower or stick-wielding primate to stockbroker, computer nerd or informed earth scientist is well documented. The most significant changes in terms of evolution include the ability to walk upright and to adapt relatively quickly to environmental change. But the ability to communicate, record and be innovative surely rank amongst the highest attributes of our species. Today with the aid of advanced technology and the outstanding developments in cellular biology we have reached a new threshold. Computers can perform billions of functions in minutes; genetic modification is the buzzword for the New Millennium. Poverty and cruelty persist however, and a large percentage of the global population will never see a hypodermic needle let alone a DNA profile of a constituent cell. The needs of the Bushmen of the Kalahari are simple, they produce very little waste or pollution. The industrial world sadly has a case to answer. It consumes colossal amounts of non-renewable resources, wastes energy, pollutes and generally sets a poor example for emergent nations to follow.

Utopia would be a world with a limited population, healthy, wealthy and very wise. The population will no doubt be genetically modified, resource management and sustainability would be the order of the day. Waste management would be extremely effective and genetic engineering could return recently extinct species to their rightful places in the biosphere.

The keys to Utopia are in our hands - will the scientist or politician prevail? Will Joe Public be ignored or remain simply uninformed? Can those concerned with the future of our planet heed the lessons of the past and plan for tomorrow. One day humankind may visit other galaxies, populate other planets and live to 150. Will Earth be the home that extraterrestrials, of human origin, want to return to? Will we survive to converse with holograms of recent ancestors or will those in power fail to use their proverbial 15 minutes of fame and fudge the future. This publication will act as a record of current thinking, some views are cataclysmic, others hopeful. Whatever happens Earth has roughly 5 billion years left of its long lifetime. Some forms such as *Lingula* have survived for over 500 my, 5 billion years would be impossible. Or would it?

THE MINERAL WORLD
Robert F. Symes FGS OBE
President Geologists' Association 1996-1998

1. Introduction

We live on a small rocky planet but how many of us really know of what the Earth is made and anything about how the minerals, the essential building blocks of the earth are formed. The mineral kingdom is in fact wonderfully varied, and by studying the properties of the various minerals and their associations it is possible to gain insight into the conditions of their formation and hence of the Earth itself

What is a mineral? What is a rock?

Virtually all the rocks, which form the Earth and Moon, are composed of minerals. Minerals are naturally occurring inorganic solids, with a definite chemical composition, and ordered atomic arrangement (structure). Rocks are natural aggregates of minerals; some rocks such as quartzite (pure quartz) and marble (pure calcite) contain only one mineral. Most however consist of more than one kind.

Minerals and Rocks

Minerals are normally classified on a chemical basis. The silicate group which comprises most of the rock forming minerals is by far the largest and most important, for we live on a silicate earth. However, there are some other important chemical groups such as the sulphides, oxides, carbonates, phosphates and sulphates.

If we look at a rock we can usually see that it is formed from several kinds of minerals. Their composition, size and texture vary according to how the rock was formed. In a hand specimen of granite we can recognise, quartz (grey areas), feldspars (white) and mica (black). If we look at these rocks in thin section under a microscope we can see much more clearly the individual rock forming minerals. The size of individual minerals may vary from a few mm in a volcanic rock to several metres in a granite pegmatite.

Rock forming processes

We live on a dynamic Earth, that is internal Earth processes are driven by the Earth's internal heat sources. These processes lead to the formation of volcanoes, mountains, continental movement and the formation of the igneous and metamorphic rocks. Surface processes driven by the Sun's energy, cause erosion, weathering and sedimentation.

Geological processes tend to work in constant cycles so that the redistribution of the chemical elements, minerals and rocks within and at the surface of the Earth is continuous (Rock Cycle) (Figure 1).

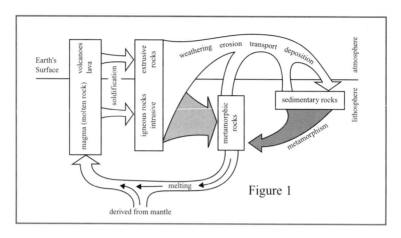

Figure 1

2. Rock Forming Minerals

Of all the chemical elements, just eight make up nearly 99% of the Earth's Crust (Figure 2). These elements combine to form naturally occurring rock forming minerals. The silicate minerals and silica are predominant in most common rocks except limestones where the carbonate minerals are predominant. We therefore, come to the classification of the rocks of the Earth - which is that all rocks are either igneous, metamorphic, or sedimentary. Igneous rocks are formed when rocks of the crust and/or mantle melt, so forming a magma which may solidify as 'intrusive' or 'extrusive' rocks. Typical intrusive rocks are granites – diorites - gabbros, and extrusive rhyolites - andesites - basalts. Igneous rocks form the greater part of the rocks of the interior of the Earth. Specific rock forming mineral groups are characteristic of certain types of igneous rocks. The minerals that form granitic rocks - quartz, feldspar, micas and amphiboles. Minerals in basalts and gabbros - plagioclase feldspars, pyroxenes and olivine.

Abundance of some chemical elements in the Earth's Crust			
Element	Percentage by weight	**Element**	Percentage by weight
oxygen	46.60	sulphur	0.05
silicon	27.72	chromium	0.02
aluminium	8.13	nickel	0.008
iron	5.00	zinc	0.0065
calcium	3.63	copper	0.0045
sodium	2.83	lead	0.0015
potassium	2.59	tin	0.0003
magnesium	2.09	silver	0.00001
titanium	0.44	platinum	0.0000005
manganese	0.10	gold	0.0000005

Figure 2

Typical rock forming minerals of sedimentary rocks are quartz (sandstone) calcite or dolomite (limestone), clays (mudstones, shales). When rocks are weathered, altered and eroded, they break down into smaller pieces of rock and new mineral products. This sediment is transported to a new site of sedimentary deposition be it river, lake or sea and deposited in layers (strata). In time these become hard rocks. The Metamorphic rocks are pre-existing rocks that have been altered by heat and/or pressure; this has usually lead to recrystallization and the formation of new minerals dependant upon the pressure/temperature regime. Such rocks contain characteristic rock forming minerals such as garnet, kyanite, staurolite, and glaucophane. If you metamorphose a limestone (calcite), the rock may be recrystallized to a marble but is still formed from the mineral calcite.

3. Journey to the Centre of the Earth

So far we have considered rocks and minerals that we see and collect at the surface of the Earth but we do know that the Earth has a layered structure and the common rocks and minerals with which we are familiar form only part of the crust of the Earth. The Earth consists of three major parts, the core, the mantle and the rigid crust (Figure 3). The Crust and upper mantle form continental and oceanic plates that move slowly over the mantle beneath. Of course the closer to the centre of the Earth the greater the pressure and temperature. The 'plates' are resting on a semi-plastic region called the Asthenosphere beneath. Of course the closer to the centre of the Earth the greater the pressure and temperature. So far our technology has only allowed us to drill a few km into the crust of the Earth, so what do we know of the minerals and rocks of the deeper Earth?

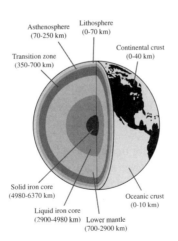

Figure 3

After Press, F. and Siever, R. 1986

Upper Mantle

The igneous rocks and the xenoliths they sometimes contain, including diamonds, can tell us a great deal about the Upper Mantle. Such xenoliths are often darkish green due to the high content of the mineral olivine and the rock is called peridotite. We believe that much of the Upper Mantle is made of peridotite.

Transition Zone and Lower Mantle

To understand the Lower Mantle and Core we have to use geophysics and computer simulation models but we do know that the minerals change in response to the increasing pressure although the composition remains similar. The main evidence for this comes from the changing velocities of earthquake waves, which indicate seismic discontinuities at 440km and 660km depth. In the deeper Earth mineralogical changes can therefore be expected as follows:

$$\text{Olivine} \quad (Mg, Fe)_2 SiO_4$$
$$\text{Orthopyroxene}$$
$$\text{440 km seismic discontinuity}$$
$$\text{Spinel} \quad (Mg, Fe)_2 SiO_4$$
$$\text{Olivine} = \text{Ringwoodite}$$
$$\text{660km seismic discontinuity}$$
$$\text{Ringwoodite} = \text{Perovskite } (Mg, Fe) SiO_3 + Mg \text{ wustite}$$

Core

Well we believe that the core is completely different in composition to the rest of the Earth rocks. There is a molten outer core (2300km radius) and inner core (1200 km) radius. Because of the terrific pressure and temperature regime (and from seismic evidence) we believe that part of the core is in a molten state (outer core). This is formed mainly of iron plus a light element such as sulphur. Temperature must be at least 4400°C the outer core is the of source the Earth's magnetic field. The solid inner core is believed to be made of nickel-iron. Maximum temperature at centre could be as high as 8000°C.

Other indirect evidence for the nature of the Core is provided by meteorites. Meteorites are rocks that fall to Earth from space and are mostly derived from the asteroid belt situated between Mars and Jupiter. Some of these are called 'iron meteorites', formed from nickel-iron and we believe these to be similar in composition to the core of the Earth.

The silicate group which comprises most of the rock forming minerals is by far the largest and most important, for we live on a silicate earth. However, another group of minerals is very important to our technology, these are the ore minerals.

4. Ore Minerals

We have been mining and quarrying the rocks and minerals of the Earth since ancient times in order to provide and improve the tools for our technology. Some minerals known as the ore minerals are the source of most useful metals. Usually in order to 'win' the metal from the ore, the minerals need to be crushed, the ore mineral separated from the gangue mineral and the product smelted.

Perhaps the first ores (mineral/rock) were flint or obsidian worked by ancient man to fashion axe-heads and tools. Advantage was then seen in working metallic minerals where they were at surface and easily quarried. The technique of smelting by fire may have been discovered accidentally but certainly led to the development of the bronze (around 3000 BC) and iron (1000 BC) ages. The Egyptians and other ancient civilisations certainly mined useful minerals and the Romans further developed mining and quarrying techniques. Lead (as the mineral galena) from the Charterhouse area of the Mendip Hills can be seen today forming part of the plumbing system in Pompeii. Surprisingly we know little of the techniques used to exploit the ore minerals in past times until the work of George Bauer 'Agricola', a German scholar. It was in 1556 that he completed his classic work 'De Re Metallica' on the mining techniques at use in Central Europe.

Most of the commercial 'ore' minerals are metallic sulphides. The 'ore' metals normally occur in only trace amounts in the Earth's crust and the metal content has to be 'concentrated' by geological processes in order to be of an economic grade. The concentrations of the metalliferous elements in ore deposits are typically a thousand times greater than average. As with many groups of minerals, the 'ore' minerals may be formed and concentrated by several geological processes, which can be of sedimentary, metamorphic or igneous origin.

Of all the mineral deposits, perhaps the most important are those formed by hydrothermal processes. As the name suggests hydrothermal solutions form and transport minerals dissolved in hot water (temperatures in the order of 100°/700°C). Such mineral deposits formed from hydrothermal solutions usually occur as vein deposits, filling cracks in the Earth's crust, or as disseminations throughout pre-existing rocks. Often the ore minerals may be further concentrated by secondary processes in the supergene environment or concentrated as alluvial deposits in modern and past drainage systems

In the British Isles we can study a variety of hydrothermal ore deposits from the galena-sphalerite-fluorites deposits of the North Pennines, the iron ore deposits of West Cumbria and of course the world famous copper, tin, tungsten deposits of Devon and Cornwall. Associated with the 'ore' minerals are the gangue minerals, which at the time of mining are not considered economic but may often form remarkably fine crystal groups.

These ore and gangue minerals can sometimes be seen to contain small inclusions of the original solutions from which they crystallized, these fluid inclusions can tell us much about the nature, composition and temperature of the original hydrothermal fluids.

Industrial Minerals

A further important group of minerals and rocks are known as the industrial minerals and again these may be formed by a variety of geological processes.

These industrial minerals are so called for they provide the raw materials for other great industries such as the chemical, paint and pigment industry and for the built environment as building stones, brick, cement and aggregate for roadstone and rail ballast.

5. Crystals

Virtually all minerals occur as crystals, maybe on the micro scale or as very large single crystals. Crystals may form from hot watery solutions, in magma, gas or sometimes in solids. All crystals grow as atoms arrange themselves, layer by layer in a regular three-dimensional network. Growth will continue to the outer surfaces until the supply stops. It is estimated that in a space of time, of say an hour, millions and millions of atoms arrange themselves layer by layer across a crystal face.

The physical state adopted by a substance depends on the temperature, pressure and volume. The states of matter may be characterised by their degrees of order and the mobility of the individual atoms.

In a crystal of a mineral the atoms are arranged in a regular pattern, entropy is low and the dense packing makes for low atomic mobility, this is the solid state.

A liquid is somewhat less ordered and the increased mobility enables it to flow and to adapt to the shape of a container.

The lowest order and thus the highest entropy are seen in the gaseous state. In gases the atoms are so widely spaced that a containing surface does not form and the substance completely fills a container.

Glasses are not in thermal equilibrium and are in a metastable state - usually formed by the rapid cooling of the corresponding liquid.

When we study crystals of minerals we are looking at the solid state and throughout time the beauty of crystals has fascinated us. The word crystal is derived from the Greek word 'kryos' meaning icy cold. In fact, a crystal is a solid with a regular internal structure. Because of the arrangement of its atoms, a crystal may form smooth external surfaces called faces. Different crystals of the same mineral may develop the same faces but the crystals may differ in size or shape. Groups of crystals may also form characteristic aggregate shapes such as the botryoidal habit of malachite (copper carbonate).

There appear to be many types of crystals but in terms of symmetry, crystals can be grouped into just seven systems, these being cubic (highest symmetry), tetragonal, orthorhombic, hexagonal, trigonal, monoclinic and triclinic (lowest symmetry).

Some chemically identical minerals exist in more than one structural state and therefore have differing properties. The element carbon for example forms the two minerals diamond (cubic) and graphite (hexagonal). Due to the differing arrangement of carbon atoms these minerals have distinctly different properties especially in their hardness, diamond being the hardest mineral known and graphite one of the softest.

No two crystals are exactly alike because the environment in which they form varies. They need space and time to develop into fine crystals - if crystallisation is rapid the crystals may be so small that they can only be seen using a microscope. One of the most interesting properties of some crystals is the piezoelectric effect. In this an alternating electric charge placed on a crystal will cause the crystal to vibrate. In a quartz watch a slice of quartz is caused to vibrate in unerring regularity, therefore keeping accurate time.

It is not surprising that natural crystals often contain impurities or have defects in some way, these defects may mean that we need to grow some crystals in the laboratory in order to make them flawless for technological use. Synthetically grown crystals may be found in almost every electronic or optical device used today.

Many minerals crystallise from hot watery solutions; from the final product we can sometimes work out a sequence of events, a first formed crystal being coated by a second and partially replaced by a third. Interruption in the growth of a crystal can produce regular inclusions, and sometimes parallel growth layers 'forming' phantom crystals

To illustrate various types of crystals we can look at some of the fine crystal groups collected from the metalliferous mines of the British Isles, for example fluorite (cubic) baryte (orthorhombic) calcite (trigonal) and cassiterite (tetragonal).

6. Gemstones

Occasionally crystals of some minerals may grow so that their colour, transparency and other properties make them useful as gemstones. We have always adorned ourselves with gemstones and decorative stones and the ancients certainly worked a range of attractive stones such as emeralds, lapis lazuli and garnets. Most gemstones are exceptional for their beauty and rarity. Usually the original mineral must be cut or fashioned to exploit their optical properties or colour. Light is reflected and refracted through gemstones so as to produce the intense colours of ruby and emerald and the 'fire' of diamond. It is the skill of the lapidary to cut diamond so that the best light path is produced causing the stone to give the 'brilliance', a spectrum of colour.

Beryl is an interesting mineral to study in terms of its use as a gemstone. It is a beryllium silicate and tends to form in granite pegmatites, or sometimes in metamorphic schists. Pure beryl is colourless (gem variety - goshenite) but the mineral has several gem varieties of different colour, emerald (green), heliodor (yellow), aquamarine (blue) and morganite (pink). These coloured varieties contain a range of trace chemical impurities, which cause the differing colours; for instance, trace managanese causes the pink variety (morganite) and chromium and vanadium, emerald.

Gemstones have to be sufficiently resistant (hardness) to survive everyday wear, say 5 or above on Mohs hardness scale. Minerals of lesser hardness may be cut and used with care. Recently fine gemstones of fluorite (calcium fluoride) have been cut but they are really too soft for everyday wear.

Precious Metals

The precious metals are gold, silver and platinum. They are attractive and easily worked and are often used as a setting for gems. Gold and silver were among the earliest metals (minerals) discovered and worked. Platinum was discovered in the mid-18th century. Gold, silver and platinum occur in a variety of geological environments; they are all rare being found in the earth's crust in very low crustal abundances (Fig. 2). Geological processes need to concentrate them to an economic grade. Gold is usually found in hydrothermal veins associated with quartz, or as nuggets in alluvial drainage systems. The largest nugget ever found was the *Welcome Stranger* from Victoria, Australia. It was found in 1869 and contained 71 kg of pure gold.

7. Minerals and Collecting

There are over 3500 different mineral species and approximately 50 new mineral species are described in the scientific literature each year most of these do not fall into the category of rock forming minerals or ore minerals but they do have a distinct new atomic structure and properties. Many of these newly described species occur only as small grains or at best in small quantities. They are not usually seen to be of great economic importance. However it is very necessary that they are studied and described for these supposedly uninteresting minerals may have new and novel atomic structures and chemistries, we are always looking for the next advance in material science. Our drab natural mineral may hide the key to a technological advance be it as a catalyst, super conductor or in case of the REE minerals enhanced strength metal alloys. A few recent examples of such minerals are given:

A. From studies of the properties of some zeolites (hydrated aluminosilicates, chiefly of sodium and calcium) they have been shown to have a framework silicate structure capable of allowing reversible ion exchange and dehydration, important in present day technology.

B. The natural oxide mineral, priderite has been shown to be important in fixing radioactive caesium within its crystal structure. Synthetically produced priderite is therefore of considerable importance in immobilizing the most dangerous component of nuclear waste. Another similar mineral redledgeite, recently described by the author can help with the immobilisation of heavy metals such as thallium in gold mining processes.

C. Recent studies of oxychloride minerals found in the Mendip Hills of Somerset have provided insight into some remarkably interesting atomic structures; interest has already been shown for technological use.

D. The mineral magnetoplumbite, a lead iron oxide was described by Aminoff in 1925 from the Langban deposit, Sweden. It is magnetic and recent studies have led to the development of synthetic similar structural magnetic analogues. These hard hexagonal ferrite magnets are used in loudspeakers, video recorders and computers.

It is often said that mineralogy is one of the few areas of science today in which a serious amateur can still make a real contribution. Most new discoveries are made ultimately by collectors sending material to museums or scientific institutions for study. While it is true that most finds will probably not lead to new technological advances, we are providing new information to the data base of natural systems, the interesting discoveries will continue to occur,

Finally along with the scientist, who studies minerals professionally, everyone can enjoy and study minerals. Some people enjoy collecting minerals as jewels or gemstones (crown!) but most collectors settle for something less sensational. Even the smallest, self collected, crystals or minerals are of interest for study. Next time you hold a mineral (crystal) look at its form and contemplate its role in Earth History.

The collecting and study of minerals is still a popular and rewarding past time.

Enjoy your world of minerals.

GEOLOGY IN THE 20th CENTURY
John F. Dewey, FGS F.R.S.
Department of Earth Sciences, University of Oxford, Parks Road Oxford, OX1 3PR

The 20th Century, especially from 1965 to 1970 has witnessed the transformation of geology from a nineteenth-century natural history discipline to a modern quantitative science. From about 1820 to 1960, the basic principles of geological history and process were laid down, mainly from meticulous and clever field observations, supplemented by analogue modelling in laboratory experiments particularly in igneous and sedimentary petrogenesis. Until about 1960, geology was based strongly in the continents. The rapid transition, during the 1960's, to modern geology resulted from the exploration of the ocean with bathymetric, dredging, gravity, heatflow, magnetic and, more recently, drilling, studies. By 1970, the basic concepts of plate tectonics were developed; a model of the earth in which, today, seven large and a few smaller, lithospheric caps or plates are in relative motion at rates of centimetres per year, in places separating to generate new surface area by sea-floor spreading in the oceans, and stretching continents to form rift valleys and extensional basins, in other places converging to subduct oceanic lithosphere in deep trenches or to form mountain belts within the continents, and to slide relatively laterally to form the great strike-slip faults such as the San Andreas and North Anatolian Faults. Generally, relative motion is oblique rather than purely orthogonal or lateral, yielding zones of transpression and transtension where oblique motion is partitioned in complicated ways into lateral and orthogonal components. It is now clear that the oceanic and continental lithospheres behave in quite different ways. The oceanic lithosphere 'turns over' by sea-floor spreading and subduction, is the main engine of global heat loss and, mostly, behaves almost perfectly rigidly according to the basic tenets of plate tectonics. The continental lithosphere, by contrast, appears to be 'non-geo-degradable' and, mainly, non-subductable because of its buoyancy and weakness; it behaves apparently as a thin weak viscous sheet with a brittle upper crust in which flakes rotate, overlap and separate to yield the typically complicated surface geology of the continents. The principles of continental plate boundary zone geology will be illustrated using New Zealand, the Alpine Ranges of Turkey and the Middle East and the Himalayas/Tibet. Modern instrumentation has played a critical part in the evolution of modern geology, notably the mass spectrometer in geochronology and isotope geology, high speed computing that allows the inversion of huge data sets in seismology, and geophysical instrumentation, especially GPS (Global Positioning Satellite) studies that allow, with seismic moment tensor sums, the development of precise velocity fields for continental plate boundary zones.

Comparative planetology has allowed, with modern studies of Archaean rocks, a re-evaluation of the early history of the earth, especially the role of holides (impacts) and crustal/upper mantle turnover/inversion. The inversion of large geophysical data sets has allowed the development of modern seismic tomography, the mapping of low viscosity/high viscosity, warmer/colder areas of the earth's mantle that, in turn, has generated new concepts of how the mantle convects and loses heat and how mantle flow patterns generate shallow and surface patterns of uplifts and basins.

Modern geochemistry, fluid dynamics and engineering geology are leading to fundamentally new concepts of chemical and physical oceanography, climatology and climate change, the weathering of the earth's crust and a new approach to quantitative environmental geology. Environmental geology is becoming, rapidly, a powerful new quantitative field of geology involving seemingly mundane, yet profoundly difficult, problems such as land stability, landfill and garbage disposal, foundation engineering geology, quarry design, and mineral exploitation. Although there will always remain the solid core of basic geological research, much of modern geology is returning to its original roots of 'geology in the service of mankind'.

The Early Earth

Monica M. Grady FGS

Department of Mineralogy, The Natural History Museum, Cromwell Road, London SW7 5BD

The oldest fossils on Earth date back to 3.5 Gyr (Schopf, 1993) and the oldest chemical traces of life back to 3.8 Gyr (Mojzsis et al., 1996). The oldest rocks are ~ 3.9 Gyr (Bowring and Housh, 1995; Nutman et al., 1997), and the oldest mineral (zircon) ~ 4.2 Gyr (Froude et al., 1983; Compston and Pidgeon, 1986). However, none of these ages represent the true age of the Earth. All traces of the original materials that came together to form the Earth have been obliterated by impact bombardment and geological processing. The formation of the Earth must be set firmly in the context of the formation of the Sun and Solar System, thus the Earth's history starts with the collapse of an interstellar molecular cloud to a protoplanetary disk (the solar nebula) and continues through a complex process of accretion, coagulation, agglomeration, melting, differentiation and solidification. Added to this are secondary influences of bombardment, collision, break-up, brecciation and re-formation. The rocks which are accessible for study at the Earth's crust are therefore not representative of the original material that accreted from the solar nebula. In order to understand the precursors of the Earth, the only relevant materials available for study in the laboratory are meteorites.

Meteorites are pieces of rock and metal that fall to the Earth and are recovered-fragments broken from asteroids, with a compositional variation that spans a whole range of planetary materials, from completely unmelted and unfractionated stony chondrites to highly fractionated and differentiated iron meteorites. These materials, and the components within them carry records of all stages of Solar System history. Study of meteorites allows more complete understanding of the processes undergone by the material that resulted in the Earth of today. The most significant meteorites, for early Solar System chronology, are the chondrites, the most primitive of all meteorites, having experienced only mild thermal or hydrothermal metamorphism since accretion into parent-bodies. Chondrites are composed of high temperature components (CAIs, chondrules) set in a matrix of fragmented chondrules mixed with minerals formed at lower temperatures. The CAIs (for Calcium, Aluminium-rich Inclusions) are refractory inclusions (up to 1 cm in size) of spinel, hibonite, melilite, etc. Chondrules are spherical to sub-spherical silicate assemblages, up to 1 mm in diameter, that have been partially or totally melted prior to parent-body accretion.

The last decade has seen a greater understanding of the processes that have led to the formation of the Sun and Solar System. Advances have resulted from astronomical observations of star formation regions in molecular clouds, the recognition and observation of protoplanetary disks and planetary systems around other stars, and also from refinement of chronologies based on short-lived radionuclides. The main stages that led to the formation of the Earth and the Solar System can be followed by the use of several different radiometric age-dating chronometers, and can be summarised as follows:

1) *Collapse of interstellar cloud and protoplanetary disk formation:* gravitational instability within an interstellar molecular cloud results in collapse of a fragment of the cloud to form a protoplanetary disk (e.g., Boss, 1989, 1993; Wetherill, 1990). The mechanism that triggers cloud collapse is not clear: several possibilities have been suggested (e.g. as a shock wave from a nearby supernova, ejection of a planetary nebula from an AGB star, Cameron, 1988), but whatever the mechanism, the collapse of the cloud and subsequent accretion of material must have been sufficiently fast to carry a complement of "live" short-lived radionuclides into the protoplanetary disk (or solar nebula). Evidence for the speed of this process comes from the presence of 26Mg (from the decay of 26Al; T1/2 ~ 0.73 Myr) within CAIs in chondritic meteorites (MacPherson et al., 1995). The occurrence of 26Mg in the inclusions shows that the CAIs formed whilst 26Al was still "live" in the solar nebula, i.e., agglomeration took place over a very short timescale, < 3 Myr (MacPherson et al., 1995). The 41Ca-41K chronometer, with T1/2 ~ 0.15 Myr, implies even more rapid formation of CAIs, with an interval between nucleosynthesis and agglomeration of < 0.3 Myr (Srinivasan et al., 1996). Absolute dating of the components within meteorites use the U-Pb isotope system, and place the date of formation of CAIs at 4566 $^{+2}_{-1}$ (Allegre et al., 1995). The most abundant component within chondrites, viz. chondrules, show little evidence for live 26Al, implying that chondrule-forming process took place, 2-3 Myr or so after the formation of CAIs (Russell et al., 1996). The growth of planet-sized bodies from micron-sized dust grains is controlled by several factors, such as the nature of the initial grains (fluffy or compact), the degree of turbulence within the nebula, and has been modelled by many authors (e.g., see Lissauer, (1993) for a review). End-member models for planetesimal formation are coagulation of material by gravitational instability in a quiescent nebula (e.g., Safronov, 1969) or by coagulation during descent to the midplane of a turbulent nebula (e.g., Weidenschilling et al., 1989; Weidenschilling and Cuzzi. 1993). The aggregation of interstellar dust ($\leq$ 0.1 µm in diameter) into increasingly large bodies, eventually forming kilometre-sized planetesimals and culminating in the asteroids and planets, took place over a time interval of some 8 Myr following formation of the CAIs (Allègre et al., 1995).

2) *Core Formation:* Once the proto-Earth had aggregated, internal heat from radioactive decay, combined with gravitational energy and collisional energy from planetesimal bombardment kept the planet molten. As the proto-Earth cooled, reduction reactions within the convecting system resulted in production of a metal-rich core and silicate-rich crust-mantle structure. The timescale over which core formation occurred can be deduced using several radiometric decay schemes, one of the most telling of which is the newly-established 182Hf-182W

chronometer (e.g., Halliday et al., 1998). The strongly lithophile 182Hf is partitioned into silicates, relative to the more siderophile W during differentiation, and subsequent variations in Hf/W are caused by decay of 182Hf to 182W (T1/2 ~ 9 Myr). Models based on the 182Hf-182W chronometer indicate that formation of the Earth's core took place gradually, some 50 Myr or so after the differentiation of iron meteorite parent-bodies (Halliday et al., 1998).

3) *Formation of the Moon:* The last event in the history of the proto-Earth was the formation of the Moon. Several mechanisms have been proposed for its formation, namely co-accretion with the Earth from the protoplanetary disk, capture of a rogue asteroid or fission from the Earth; these mechanisms are reviewed by Wood (1986). The hypothesis that is now the most widely-accepted (Newsom and Taylor, 1989) is that suggested independently by Hartmann and Davis (1975) and Cameron and Ward (1976), in which a Mars-sized body collides with the Earth. Refinements of this hypothesis indicate that the impact occurred after the Earth's core had formed, and that the crust-mantle regions of both the impactor and the proto-Earth were vaporised then mixed during the impact (Melosh, 1990). This hypothesis accounts satisfactorily for the geochemical, mineralogical and isotopic compositions of the lunar samples as represented by material returned by Apollo and Luna missions. The timing of the giant impact event is set at around 4.51 Gyr (Lee et al., 1997).

Following from the giant impact that formed the Moon, the Earth suffered a prolonged period of bombardment by smaller projectiles. Although no trace of this bombardment remains on the Earth's surface, having been erased by subsequent geological processing, the scars are visible to be seen as craters on the Moon's surface. This epoch of bombardment lasted until ~ 3.9Gyr, and gradually decreased over 400 Myr to 3.5Gyr, as determined by the relative crater counting on the Moon (Grieve, 1988). It is likely that in this interval, the Earth's atmosphere and oceans might have been produced and lost several times, along with any developing life (Sleep et al., 1989). The evolution of Earth's atmosphere to the oxidising composition of today, took until 2.2 Gyr to achieve (Kasting, 1993), and an additional ~ 1.6 Gyr were to pass before the explosion in biodiversity at the start of the Cambrian period (~ 570 Myr ago). Thus a history of the early Earth spans some 4000 Myr, from its birth in an interstellar cloud, to its colonisation by multi-cellular species.

References

C.J. Allègre, G. Manhès and C. Gopel. The age of the Earth. *Geochim. Cosmochim. Acta* 59, 1445-1456 (1995).

A.P. Boss. Evolution of the solar nebula - I. Nonaxisymmetric structure during nebula formation. *Ap. J.* 345, 554-571 (1989).

A.P. Boss. Evolution of the solar nebula - II. Thermal structure during nebula formation. *Ap. J.* 417, 351-367 (1993).

S.A. Bowring and T. Housh. The Earth's early evolution. *Science* 269, 1535-1540 (1995).

A.G. W. Cameron. Origin of the Solar System. *Ann. Rev. Astron. Astrophys.* 26, 441 - 472 (1988).

A.G. W. Cameron and W. R. Ward. The origin of the Moon. *Linar Planet. Sci. Conf. VII*, 120-122 (1976).

W. Compston and R. T. Pidgeon. Jack Hills, evidence of more very old detrital zircons in Western Australia. *Nature 321*, 766-769 (1983).

D.O. Froude, T. R. Ireland, P. D. Kinny, I. S. Williams and W. Compston. Ion microprobe identification of 4,100 - 4,200 Myr-old terrestrial zircons. *Nature 304*, 616-618 (1986).

R.A. F. Grieve. Extraterrestrial impacts on Earth: the evidence and the consequences. *In: Meteorites: Flux with Time and Impact Effects (ed. M. M. Grady et al.). Geol. Soc. London. Sp. Pub. 140*, 105-131 (1998).

A.N. Halliday, D.-C. Lee, J. N. Christensen, M. Rehkämper, W. Yi, X. Luo, C. M. Hall, C. J. Ballentine, T. Pettke and C. Stirling. Applications of multiple-collector-ICPMS to cosmochemistry, geochemistry and paleoceanography. *Geochim. Cosmochim. Acta 62*, 9 19-940 (1998).

W. K. Hartmann and D. R. Davis. Satellite-sized planetesimals and lunar origin. *Icarus* 24, 504-515 (1975).

J.F. Kasting. Earth's early atmosphere. *Science* 259, 920-926 (1993).

D.-C. Lee, A. N. Halliday, G. A. Snyder and L. A. Taylor. Age and origin of the Moon. *Science 278*, 1098 – 1103 (1997).

J. L. Lissauer. Planet formation. *Ann. Rev. Astron. Astrophys.* 31, 129-174 (1993).

G. J. MacPherson, A. M. Davis and E. K. Zinner. The distribution of aluminum-26 in the early Solar System - a reappraisal. *Meteoritics 30*, 365-386 (1995).

H. J. Melosh. Giant impacts and the thermal state of the early Earth. In: *Origin of the Earth*, ed. H.E. Newsom & J.H.J. Jones, O.U. P. 69-83 (1990).

S. J. Mojszis, G. Arrhenius, K. D. McKeegan, T. M. Harrison, A. P. Nutman and C. R. L. Friend. Evidence for life on Earth before 3,800 million years ago. *Nature 385*, 55-59 (1996).

H. E. Newsom and S. R. Taylor. Geochemical implications of the formation of the Moon by a single giant impact. *Nature 338*, 29-34 (1989).

A. P. Nutman, S. J. Mojzsis and C. R. L. Friend. Recognition of 3,850Ma water-lain sediments in West Greenland and their significance for the early Archaean Earth. *Geochim. Cosmochim. Acta 61*, 2475-2484 (1997).

S. S. Russell, G. Srinivasan, G. R. Huss, G. J. Wasserburg and G. J. MacPherson. Evidence for widespread 26A1 in the solar nebula and constraints for nebula timescales. *Science 273*, 757-762 (1996).

V. S. Safronov. Evolution of the Protoplanetary Cloud and Formation of the Earth and Planets. Moscow: Nauka. Transl. by IPST in 1972 as *NASA TTF-677* (1969).

J. W. Schopf. Microfossils of the early Archaean Apex chert: new evidence for the antiquity of life. *Science 260*, 640-646 (1993).

N. H. Sleep, K. J. Zahnle, J. F. Kasting and H. J. Horowitz. Annihilation of ecosystems by large asteroid impacts on the early Earth. *Nature 342*, 139-142 (1989).

G. Srinivasan, S. Sahijpal, A. A. Ulyanov and J. N. Goswami. Ion microprobe studies of Efremovka CAIs: II. Potassium isotope composition and 41Ca in the early Solar System. *Geochim. Cosmochim. Acta 60*, 1823-1835 (1996).

S. J. Weidenschilling and J. N. Cuzzi. In: *Protostars and Planets III* (ed. L.H. Levy & J.L. Lunine). Univ. Arizona Press. (1993).

S. J. Weidenschilling, B. Donn and P. Meakin. Physics of planetesimal formation. In: *The Formation and Evolution of Planetary Systems* (ed. H.A. Weaver & L. Danly). C. U. P. 131-150 (1989).

G. W. Wetherill. Formation of the Earth. *Ann. Rev. Earth Planet. Sci. 18*, 205-256 (1990).

J. A. Wood. (1986). In: *Origin of the Moon* (ed. W.K. Hartmann et al.). LPI. 609- (1986).

FLUIDS AND THE EVOLUTION OF THE EARTH

Marian B. Holness FGS

Department of Earth Sciences, University of Cambridge, Downing Street, Cambridge CB2 3EQ

1. Introduction

Fluids of some kind are common everywhere within the Earth. The most familiar are probably water, oil and gas, all of which can be obtained by drilling holes into rock formations which contain them, known respectively as aquifers and oil (or gas) reservoirs. Perhaps less familiar, or less obvious, are the fluids found much deeper in the Earth. These fluids include molten rock (also known as magma or, if it is erupted at the Earth's surface, as lava), and complex mixtures of water, carbon dioxide, ammonia, carbon monoxide and brine. The movement of fluids within the Earth since the very earliest stages of its history have had a tremendous impact on the way the Earth has evolved as a planet into a body containing well defined divisions of core, mantle. crust and hydrosphere.

2. The importance of fluid flow in determining the evolution of the Earth

Before the beginning of the geological record, about 4.7 billion years ago, our planet began to grow by the accretion of planetesimals, forming a homogeneous mixture of silicon compounds. iron and magnesium oxides and smaller amounts of other elements. Although the individual planetesimals were cold, the potential energy released on accretion and the gravitational energy supplied by the collapse of the accreting mass served to increase the temperature within the growing proto-planet. The temperature was further increased by the radioactive decay of the heavy elements uranium, thorium and the heavy isotopes of potassium. Using informed guesses about the temperature and the amount of radioactivity in the early Earth it seems probable than when the Earth was less than a billion years old its temperature increased to the point at which iron melts. This had profound consequences for the evolution of the planet. Iron is a heavy element and, once it had begun to melt, would have fallen towards the centre of the planet, displacing the lighter material upwards. The movement of large quantities of liquid iron to form the Earth's core was thus the first stage in the differentiation of the planet into the complex structure we are familiar with today. Since about a third of the planet's mass is iron, the gravitational energy released by the movement of liquid iron to the planet's centre act ed to further increase the temperature within the Earth to values of perhaps 2000oC. at which point the rest of the planet began to melt too, further progressing the differentiation process. Liquid rock is lighter than the solid material from which it is derived and so the magma would have risen upwards to the surface and solidified to form a primitive form of crust. The planet would then have been transformed from a homogeneous body to a concentrically zoned body with a dense core, a crust made of light, low melting point material. and between them the mantle (Figure I).

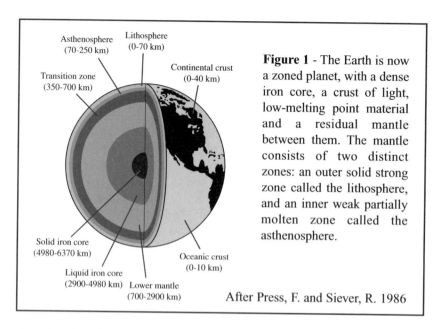

Figure 1 - The Earth is now a zoned planet, with a dense iron core, a crust of light, low-melting point material and a residual mantle between them. The mantle consists of two distinct zones: an outer solid strong zone called the lithosphere, and an inner weak partially molten zone called the asthenosphere.

After Press, F. and Siever, R. 1986

Water has also played a major role in the chemical differentiation of the planet. Starting from the premise that the Earth formed by the accretion of cold planetesimals, all the water now found in the oceans came from the interior. Originally the water was bound up in the crystal lattice of minerals such as micas and amphiboles, but as the Earth warmed and melted this water was released into the magma and carried upwards to the surface. Here it escaped from the lava carrying it and formed vapour clouds. This kind of "outgassing" process is also believed to have resulted in the formation of the atmosphere, with erupting magmas giving up their load of dissolved hydrogen, hydrogen chloride, carbon dioxide and nitrogen at the Earth's surface. Furthermore, the addition of water to previously dry hot rock can promote melting. Again since liquid rock will move upwards this can contribute to the differentiation process.

Chemical differentiation is still going on, although not with quite the same catastrophic effects that the onset of melting of the iron would have had. The composition of today's crust is very different from that of the first crust, with considerable enrichment of aluminium, silica and the heavy elements uranium and thorium, due to the continued movement of magma upwards through the residual, heavier, solid material. Additionally, the arrival of hot magma at high levels in the Earth's crust results in metamorphism of the lower temperature rocks it comes into contact with, and this can result in small-scale differentiation as water and carbon dioxide bound up in crustal rocks are released by the breakdown of the low temperature minerals. These volatile fluids move upwards, often carrying dissolved material and affecting the development of the rocks through which they pass.

To understand the workings and development of the complex machine represented by our planet we need to understand how it is that liquids can move through what might appear to the uninitiated to be solid rock.

3. Flow through solids

In order to move fluids through any solid material, pore space has to be created. Pore space. also known as porosity, is what we call the empty space in a solid, which a fluid can occupy. The more porosity in a rock, the more fluid it can hold. The actual amount of porosity in a rock is not the whole story however, as movement of a fluid requires that the pore space be interconnected so that a throughway can be found. The extent of connection between the individual pore spaces within a rock is described by the permeability, which tells us how easy it is for the fluid to move through under the influence of a hydrostatic gradient. If we want to understand how fluids of any kind move through rocks we need to know about the amount and the extent of connectedness of pore space.

Familiar forms of pore space include cracks and fractures, gaps between individual grains in a sedimentary rock and, on a much larger scale, cave systems. These cannot be the whole picture however. At great depths within the Earth, large cave systems and major open fractures would simply collapse under the pressure of the overlying rock, squeezing upwards any fluid they contain. This is because hot rocks can continually re-form their constituent crystal grains under the influence of high stresses, and this has profound effects on the possible pathways for fluid flow.

To understand the way fluids can flow through rock at any temperature we need to think about a variety of different processes, such as crystal growth, textural equilibration, reactions between minerals and fluids, and the influence of deformation, each of which contribute to the amount, shape and development of porosity.

(i) Crystal growth/dissolution

The growth of crystals occurs during reactions, such as the solidification of a liquid (e.g. water freezing to form ice crystals), the precipitation of minerals from liquid as their solubility is decreased, and also the formation of a new set of stable minerals from a pre-existing unstable assemblage during metamorphism. The shape of the resultant crystals is controlled by the relative rates of growth of different crystal faces which is strongly influenced by the growth environment. A single mineral, such as calcite ($CaCO_3$), can form a wide range of different crystal shapes depending on the conditions of growth, although the different shapes are related through the underlying symmetry of the crystal lattice.

The opposite process, crystal dissolution, is not the exact reverse of growth, even for the same mineral in the same environment. This is because dissolution tends to occur fastest at points in the crystal lattice which have higher energy, due to the presence of mistakes in the lattice or grain boundaries.

The amount of pore space in a rock is affected by the growth or dissolution of crystals. The exact shape of the growing or shrinking crystals controls the pore connectivity, and hence the permeability, of the porous rock (Figure 2).

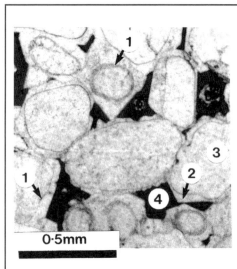

Figure 2 - A thin section through a porous sandstone showing the pore space as black (4), and the quartz grains as pale grey. The original shape of these detrital grains (3) is outlined by a fine line of fine-grained dark material (1) and the overgrowth of cement (2) can be clearly seen. The way the pore space will evolve during the cementation process will depend on the crystal shapes taken by the cement.

After Cooper, M.R. and Hunter, R.H. 1995

(ii) Textural equilibration (Figure 3)

Textural equilibration is the process which results in liquid drops becoming spherical and the amalgamation of isolated spherical drops of oil in a simple salad dressing. This kind of thing also happens (but much more slowly) in solid materials and is driven by the reduction in energy which can be achieved by decreasing the area of grain boundaries and interfaces, both of which have energy associated with them (analogous to the surface tension of liquid drops). Rocks containing fluid not only contain grain boundaries but also interfaces between the solid minerals and the fluid phase. If the fluid-bearing porous material can undergo textural equilibration then the pore shape and connectivity can be predicted if we know the value of the porosity and the relative values of the energy associated with grain boundaries and fluid-solid interfaces.

Textural equilibration is a slow process and is only important at the high temperatures found in high-grade metamorphic rocks and igneous rocks.

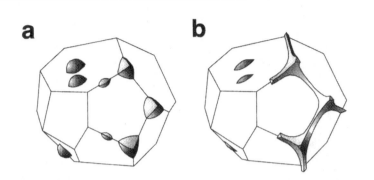

Figure 3 - The two possible forms the porosity will take in texturally equilibrated fluid-bearing materials. a) the pores are all isolated and occur at the junctions between 3 and 4 grains; b) the pore space forms an entirely interconnected network along 3-grain junctions.

After Watson, E.B., and Brenan, J.M. 1987

(iii) Reaction-controlled porosity

Mineral reactions, such as those which occur in metamorphic rocks, often result in a change of the total volume of the material present. If the total volume of solids is decreased then this can result in the formation of pore space which survives until it is compacted out by the weight of the overlying rock.

A similar change in volume often accompanies melting reactions. The melting of wet crustal rocks is generally accompanied by a decrease in total volume but the dry melting reaction has the opposite effect. The volume of residual material + melt in dry systems is greater than that of the starting material and the increase in volume can result in the formation of melt-filled cracks as the overpressured system tries to expand.

The movement of melt is greatly facilitated by the presence of these cracks which may be an important factor in moving crustally-derived magmas from their source regions.

(iv) Deformation-enhanced fluid flow

The Earth is a dynamic system and rocks are almost continually in a state of stress. The resultant deformation can have a profound effect on rock permeability. Fracturing can concentrate fluid flow into discrete channelways and often results in the formation of mineral-filled veins. At higher temperatures the rock may start to behave as a ductile material instead of suffering brittle failure. In this case the pore structure becomes one of elongate aligned pores, and connectivity and flow become possible even in materials in which the texturally equilibrated pore structure is an impermeable one.

The actual form of the porosity and the ease with which fluids can move through rocks is going to be controlled by all four of the above processes, each of which act in parallel. At any one time the pore structure is going to be determined by the relative importance of each of the four processes. The balance between them will be controlled by the temperature, the stress field, and the rate of reaction.

For example, in low temperature sedimentary rocks which form the reservoirs for hydrocarbons, reservoir pore structure and permeability will be controlled by the amount and type of cementation (i.e. the crystals precipitated in the pore space) and the number and spacing of pre-existing fractures and faults in the rock. Temperatures are far too low to permit textural equilibration to play any role.

In contrast, at the high temperatures found in solidifying magma chambers, the melt-filled porosity will be controlled by the balance between the competing processes of crystal growth and textural equilibration.

In the mantle, the movement of melts will occur in pore space which is controlled by the balance between textural equilibration and the effects of ductile deformation associated with mantle convection.

Research into the balancing act between the four separate processes described above can be applied to the various environments in which fluids move through rocks by changing variables such as fluid and rock composition, pressure and temperature. From this we can deduce the mechanisms and rates relevant to each fluid flow event and begin to understand just how it was that the early homogeneous Earth became the structurally complex planet we know today.

4. Acknowledgements

Fig. 1 - Press F. and Siever, R. 1986 *Earth*. Freeman, N.Y.

Fig. 2 - Cooper, M.R. and Hunter, R.H. 1995 *Mineralogical Magazine, 59*, 2 13-20.

Fig. 3 - Watson, E.B. and Brenan, J.M. 1987 *Earth and Planetary Science Letters, 85*, 497-5 15.

MINERALS AND THE NATURAL ENVIRONMENT - THE FOUNDATION OF WEALTH

Jane A Plant FGS CBE
BGS, Keyworth, Nottingham NG12 5GG

1. Introduction

World consumption of minerals, including oil, coal and water, is increasing steadily. It is likely to continue to increase if the expectations of Asia, Central and South America, and Africa are to be met. At the same time, there is growing concern that the development and use of mineral and other natural resources at current rates is unsustainable. The environment, too, is subject to damage from human activities because of inadequate understanding, process control and management, and environmental economics indicates that pollution and waste will limit growth more effectively than the availability of resources. The presentation will review some of the properties of energy, metallic and non-metallic minerals, with specific reference to minerals extraction in Britain, and consider new technologies that are needed to improve the environmental performance of the industry into the twenty-first century, with particular reference to the contribution that geologists can make.

Sustainable development, including the sustainable use of all resources, has become a central policy objective of most Governments. In economic terms, the total resource base is the aggregate of produced, human and natural capital (including raw materials, waste receptors, landscape and amenity assets). Sustainability requires a non-declining capital stock over time accompanied by economic efficiency, fairness across different interest groups, and caution in dealing with risk and uncertainty.

Britain is fortunate in being well endowed with a wide range of mineral resources upon which a large and diverse extractive industry of considerable economic importance is based. The value of major sectors of the minerals extractive industry is shown in Table 1: together with the mineral-based sectors of electricity generation, manufacturing and construction, this contributed £70 billion to the economy or 10.8% of GDP in 1996. Additional contributions are made from metals and minerals trading, consultancy, communication and training, estimated at a further £2 billion a year.

Table 1. Value of United Kingdom mineral production - 1996-1997
£ million

	1996	1997
Oil and natural gas liquids	12599	11027
Natural gas	5295	5254
Coal	1768	1636
Industrial and construction minerals	2150	2347
Metalliferous minerals	9	8
Total	**21821**	**20272**

Source: UK Minerals Yearbook, British Geological Survey

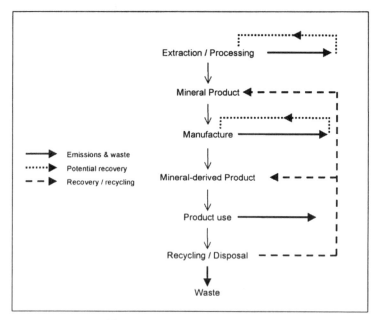

Figure 1 - Life cycle of a mineral

Figure 2. Life cycle of mineral-bearing land

        Mineral Exploration
        ↓
        Mineral Resource / Reserve
        ↓
        Mineral Extraction
        ↓
        Restoration
        ↓
        Re-use

(Agriculture, nature conservation, forestry, amenity, residential, industrial)

2. Technology Development and the Minerals Life Cycle (Figures 1, 2)

Resource Assessment and Exploration Methods

The location of mineral workings is dictated primarily by geological factors ("Minerals are where you find them") in contrast to most other forms of economic development where socio-economic issues predominate. This is particularly true for high-value deposits, but less so for bulk materials such as aggregates for which development depends on local needs and transport costs.

Environmental considerations are becoming a major constraint on mineral development worldwide. Mineral extraction in the UK, for example, is almost always restricted by planning designations and decisions rather than resource limitations. Moreover, many valuable resources have been, and continue to be, sterilised by uninformed development.

In order to provide a basis for optimum land-use planning and informed policy for sustainable development, the nation's mineral resources should be identified as fully as possible. The databases and information technologies developed should be made available to the minerals industry and to all those concerned with natural resource and environmental development, management and planning. New methods required for the identification of resources of minerals, hydrocarbons and water include:

- Remote sensing, airborne surveys and other geophysical and geochemical methods, especially new methods such as electrokinetic and three and four dimensional seismic surveys, and microchemical methods of analysis.

- Metallogenic economic and environmental models to develop criteria which can be used to interrogate spatial databases to identify natural (including deeply buried) resources and potential environmental hazards.

- Development of neural networks and decision support systems for multi-dataset integration and analysis using standardised databases.

- New, low-cost, high-productivity, methods for determining organic species in natural materials, for both the exploration and environmental industries (comparable to the methods increasingly available for inorganic substances).

- New in-situ analytical methods for organic and inorganic mineral and chemical substances.

- Comparative ecological/economic assessment methodologies, particularly for aggregates onshore and for coastal and marine sand and gravel recovery.

- Novel drilling techniques, such as small-scale rigs and horizontal, low-angle, extended- reach drilling

- Improvements in three-dimensional modelling and analysis based on advanced computer software for the delineation of resources, including mineral deposits, and the development of sustainable extraction methods

Mineral Extraction and Processing

Mineral extraction and processing are primary industries with well-established and mature technologies, but there are considerable opportunities for new developments. New mineral-processing technologies will underpin the success and sustainability of the UK-owned minerals and extractive industries worldwide and should be aimed particularly at reducing environmental damage and energy consumption. They should include:

- Automation of mining and quarrying, including increased use of computer models to improve safety and mineral-recovery ratios.

- Improvements in rock-breaking and mineral-liberation techniques.

- Biohydrometallurgy and bioextraction, especially the development of more specific and temperature-resistant bacterial strains to allow wider and environmentally more acceptable applications for non-intrusive mining and both in-situ and heap leaching.

- New technologies for the extraction of minerals from marine environments.

- Sensor development to improve the monitoring and control of extraction processes.

- Improved technology for ultra-fine (<10μm) mineral processing. This will involve greater understanding of the kinetics of physico-chemical separation processes for clay minerals and base metals in order to improve recovery and reduce environmental damage and energy consumption.

- Development of new and improved separation techniques to recover minerals from secondary sources, such as contaminated land and offshore dredgings.

- Better understanding of clay technology and potential in structural products (eg bricks and tiles) and industrial processes (kaolin), as well as engineering and construction.

- Methods to enhance the yield and recovery of hydrocarbons from oilfields.

Metal Extraction and Processing

Many metal-extraction processes are based on concepts first developed several decades ago but made significantly more efficient by incremental improvements. However, with the increasing demand for metals of the highest purity and the need to minimise energy consumption and pollution, there are many opportunities for innovative technologies concerned with control, waste minimisation and clean technology. The examples discussed below should have a very significant impact on improving extraction processes.

Sensor Technology

Several pyrometallurgical processes are more efficient by several orders of magnitude than they were 20 or 30 years ago. For example 400 tonnes of steel can now be refined in 20 minutes as opposed to 12 hours in the 1950s. This has been brought about by a greater understanding of heat and mass transfer and the use of materials able to withstand higher temperatures and more corrosive conditions. The speed of analysis of the melts is too slow and there are many examples of process trains in which chemical analysis is only of retrospective use. On-line sensors are needed urgently for the rapid determination of impurities (Table 2).

Table 2. - Process Impurities

Process	Impurities
Iron and steel	sulphur, phosphorus, nitrogen
Zinc	arsenic, antimony, sodium, aluminium
Copper	oxygen, arsenic, phosphorus
Aluminium	sodium, hydrogen, magnesium
Lead	arsenic, antimony, bismuth, silver

Apart from oxygen (which is not determined), these elements are normally analysed by traditional methods. On-line analysis would enable processes to be more efficient and less polluting, and minimise energy usage. As well as analysis of solutes in molten metals, sensors are also required to monitor off-take gases such as SO_x, NO_x, HCL, Hg, HF, so that remedial action can be taken.

New Processes

Many impurities are removed from molten metals by the addition of reactive elements to form compounds which become stabilised in a slag phase. The efficiency and profitability of metal refining could be greatly improved and its environmental impact reduced by removal of the impurities in a pure form. Potentially useful techniques include:

- microwave and ultrasound processing;

- electro-refining;

- vapour phase partitioning/extraction;

- crystallisation;

- separation processes based on physical parameters such as particle size, mineral density, surface charge density;

Although the steel industry is the world's largest recycler, it is nevertheless important to examine additional ways of treating used consumer products and the residues created during steel processing. New technologies such as electro-refining and metal refining by intercalation merit examination.

Recycling, Waste Streams and By-products

England and Wales produce about 122 million tonnes of controlled waste (commercial, industrial, municipal and construction and demolition waste) annually, of which about 70% is disposed of in landfill sites. In addition, UK mining and quarrying, and agriculture produce 110 and 80 million tonnes of waste per annum respectively. New technologies will be required to increase the amount of material recycled and of by-products recovered, in order to reduce environmental impact. Such development will complement the government's 'Sustainable Development Strategy'. Many process residues contain potentially valuable materials which could be recovered with the aim of discharging only clean air, water or inert matter into the environment.

A cost-benefit balance between recycling schemes and a range of disposal options is required. Recycling is not necessarily a costless and environmentally benign activity, and different disposal options including landfill, incineration and composting - all entail different financial costs and environmental impacts.

Many current waste streams could be minimised or re-used, adding value and reducing the need for disposal. Developments which would be of most direct benefit include:

- Review of aggregate specifications, e.g. for road building, and the development of new technologies for the treatment and grading of aggregates from secondary sources, including in-situ reprocessing as laid out in the DoE report 'Use of Waste and Recycled Materials as Aggregates', and by the DoE commissioned Aggregates Advisory Service.

- New value-added products derived from 'waste' materials such as slags and residues. These will require support by a computer database system designed to match available 'waste' to user needs.

- Methods for the recovery and reuse of materials using physical, chemical and bio-leaching technologies from waste streams including spoil from mine and mineral working, landfilled material and sewage sludge.

- Methods to promote the yield of by-products during energy extraction, as well as from cooling systems, to 'minimise discharges to the environment and increase economic returns, such as the recovery of coal impurities during burning.

- Methods for treating the by-products of oil and gas production, such as oily drill cuttings, to standards appropriate for re-use or safe discharge, including discharge to the marine environment.

- Understanding of the conditions under which toxins such as certain dioxins and PCBs form and decompose during incineration and other waste-treatment processes.

- Methods for recycling beach materials for coastal defence.

- Methods for injecting carbon dioxide and unwanted fluid products into exhausted hydrocarbon reservoirs.

In addition to conventional recycling, innovative schemes are required which combine waste from disparate industries to produce new products or chemicals. It is also important to address the problem of the ease of recycling after use, so as not to design artefacts consisting of intimate mixtures of materials and elements which cannot be recycled or separated.

Land Remediation and Aftercare

Although modern industry seeks to minimise contaminating discharges there remains a stock of land affected by previous use. Such land should be recycled and re-used as far as possible. Permission to extract minerals is conditional on land being restored to a state suitable for subsequent beneficial afteruse. When mineral working is complete the remaining voids can themselves have considerable value, sometimes exceeding that of the material extracted. Potential uses include leisure activities, agriculture, nature conservation and landfill.

The remediation of mineral workings or contaminated land must be planned carefully to meet environmental requirements efficiently and effectively. A remediated site should reach stability as quickly as possible, to minimise the need for aftercare. Developments required include:

- Spatial databases designed to identify contamination of soil and water (as well as air) with neural network and decision support system methods to evaluate potential impacts based on risk analysis.

- Integrated environmental management techniques, involving the full cycle of control, treatment and monitoring, and incorporating control sensor systems to stabilise contaminated areas and minimise emissions from them to water, land/soil and air.

- Botanical, microbiological, fungal and genetically based bio-remediation techniques, including bio-extraction, with optimisation of nutrient supply and hydraulic regimes and their use to promote accelerated growth of organisms.

- Recovery of minerals, base and radioactive metals, and other chemicals using eg biological and chemical heap leaching methods.

- Means to enable landfill and mine gases, especially methane, to be collected, processed and used more extensively and efficiently.

- Means to protect available water resources, and treat or segregate polluted waters (e.g. acid mine drainage). Where possible, such treatment should lead to the recovery of by--products in potentially usable form.

- Real-time systems for monitoring the management and remediation of contaminated land, including genetically modified organisms and electronic sensor systems. Such systems could also be used in initial investigation and assessment and have broad generic applications.

- Baseline, monitoring and modelling studies of contaminants in soil, fresh water, estuarine and marine environments, to minimise environmental impacts.

- Whole-life planning of production and extraction facilities, such as mines and on- and off-shore oil rigs, to include methods for decommissioning, recycling of materials, minimising post-extraction subsidence, etc.

3. Into the Future

The concept of sustainable development, with its requirement to maximise the value of the original mineral resource, is concerned with the global use and availability of mineral raw materials. It also has much to do with managing mineral development at a local level in such a way that a beneficial legacy - diversified economic activity (manufacturing, farming, new mines), education, skills development, public health and rehabilitated or re-utilised landscapes reflecting local needs -- remains after the mineral is exhausted.

The UK's natural-resource and environment industries, which include many of Britain's most profitable international companies, have an excellent record of continuous technological progress and improvement and of marketing their skills worldwide. The sector has the potential to contribute further to wealth creation, quality of life and sustainable development, provided that new technologies for natural resource and environmental management are continuously developed. It is essential that geologists are fully involved in developing and applying the new science and technology that will be required to take these industries into the new millennium.

Preludes to the Phanerozoic: major transitions in the early evolution of life on Earth

Nicholas J. Butterfield

Department of Earth Sciences, University of Cambridge, Cambridge CB2 3EQ

Geological time is divided into two great parts. The Phanerozoic, comprising the most recent 540 million years, is characterised by the abundant and conspicuous occurrence of fossils. By contrast, the preceding four billion years of the Precambrian present a fundamentally more elusive record, not only because of the pervasive recycling of older rocks, but also the dearth of large, readily fossilised organisms. Nevertheless, it is this earlier interval that witnessed most of life's major transitions, from the origin of life itself to the evolution of eukaryotes (organisms with nucleated cells), multicellularity, and animals. It thus warrants special attention.

The most important biological transition was surely that which first introduced life on Earth, and it is here that Precambrian palaeontology has contributed its most profound discovery – that life appeared on Earth remarkably early, probably as early as was physically possible. The oldest unambiguous evidence of life on the planet is found in the oldest well preserved sedimentary rocks on Earth, the 3.5 billion year old Warrawoona Group of Western Australia. In addition to the occurrence of stromatolites - layered structures interpreted as the trace fossils of microbial mats - microscopic examination of these early Archean rocks has revealed a range of unicellular and filamentous microfossils comparable to modern cyanobacteria. Perhaps most significantly, carbon isotopic (geochemical) signatures of the Warrawoona sediments indicate the very early establishment of green-plant photosynthesis. The consequent production of molecular oxygen would have been a critical factor in modifying and modulating the early terrestrial environment.

The oldest recognisable sedimentary rocks on Earth are from the 3.8 billion year old Isua Supracrustal sequence of SW Greenland. Although severely altered by subsequent metamorphism, carbon isotopic analyses of these metasediments still suggest the presence of photosynthesis-based life. Significantly, regular sterilisation of the early Earth by heavy meteorite bombardment appears to have continued up until four billion years ago, leaving no more than 200 million years for the evolution, or introduction, of life on Earth.

All evidence points to the earliest life forms having a prokaryotic grade of organisation. It is the eukaryotes, however, that account for the majority of modern diversity, including all the large complex organisms of the Phanerozoic. The earliest record of eukaryotic life is recorded by a diagnostic biomarker molecule (chemical fossil) recently extracted from late Archean (2700 Ma) sediments of the Fortescue Group, in Western Australia. Preserved body fossils of eukaryotes, however, are first encountered much later, in Palaeoproterozoic rocks (ca. 1900 Ma) from China. Although these single-celled microfossils - so-called acritarchs (Figure 1) - are not assignable to any particular taxonomic group, their relatively large size (0.01-1.0 mm) identifies them as bona fide eukaryotes. Despite its early appearance, the diversity and abundance of eukaryotic life remained conspicuously low until the latter part of the Mesoproterozoic, suggesting they contributed little to early Precambrian ecology or environments.

Beginning around 1300 to 1000 million years ago there is a marked rise in eukaryotic diversity with the appearance of conspicuously ornamented acritarchs, multicellular seaweeds (red, green and "brown" algae), and numerous problematic forms. Combined with molecular phylogenetic evidence for a major diversification of eukaryotic kingdoms relatively late in their history, this late Mesoproterozoic to early Neoproterozoic spike in fossil diversity has been dubbed the "Big Bang" of eukaryotic evolution. But why the ca. 1500 million year delay from their first appearance?

Most modern eukaryotes reproduce sexually and it has been suggested that it was the evolution of sex that induced the "Big Bang". Certainly the first fossil evidence of sex is found at this time, in populations of a 1200 million year old filamentous red alga, *Bangiomorpha pubescens* (Figure 1.4), which include two distinct spore-producing habits. The conventional view holds that sex contributed primarily through its accompanying genetic recombination. There is, however, an alternative possibility based on the argument that sex was a prerequisite for the evolution of complex multicellularity (Buss 1988, The Evolution of Individuality, Princeton University Press). As the source of most organismal morphology, including large size, this new multicellular grade of organisation would have introduced a critical new factor to the evolutionary process, triggering a positive feedback loop of increasingly complex morphology, ecology and evolution. For what it is worth, sexually reproducing *Bangiomorpha* represents the first documented occurrence of complex multicellularity.

Eukaryotic diversity and morphology shows a general increase through the ca. 500 million years of the Neoproterozoic (1000–543 Ma), including the appearance of macroscopic animals in its terminal 20–30 million years. I suggest that this progressive phase of eukaryote evolution began late in the Mesoproterozoic with the "invention" of a directional, coevolutionary, biological environment based on organism morphology. By contrast, the earlier prokaryote-dominated biosphere operated almost entirely in response to simple physical environments with little indication of directional biological evolution. Even so, these earlier life forms did induce critical unidirectional changes in early environments, simply through the additive effects of their metabolisms, not least an increasingly oxygen-rich atmosphere. It was these biogeochemically modified environments that paved the way for eukaryotes, multicellularity (Figure 1.1) and the Phanerozoic radiation of large complex organisms.

Figure 1. Captions

1.1: *Bangiomorpha pubescens* from the 1200 Ma Hunting Formation, Somerset Island, arctic Canada. This is the oldest taxonomically resolved eukaryote on record. It is also represents the oldest known occurrence of sexual reproduction and complex multicellularity.

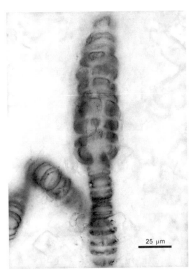

1.2: Illustration of a sphaeromorphic acritarch of the type that first appears at ca. 1850 Ma and, on the basis of its relatively large size is accepted as a bona fide eukaryote. It's from 850 Ma old shales of the Wynniatt Formation, Victoria Island, arctic Canada.

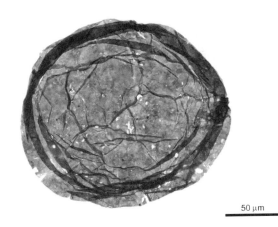

1.3: An acanthomorphic or ornamented acritarch, of the type that first appears around the Mesoproterozoic-Neoproterozoic boundary (1000 Ma). These record the onset of the so-called "big bang" of eukaryotic evolution where many of the modern kingdoms put in their first appearance. This specimen is from the 850 Ma Wynniatt Formation, Victoria Island, arctic Canada.

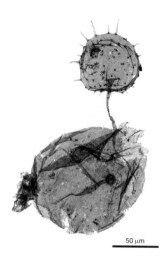

1.4: *Valkyria borealis*, a problematic multicelluar fossil showing at least 6 distinct "cell types" from the 750 Ma Svanbergfjellet Formation, Spitsbergen. This is the most complex fossil known of this age.

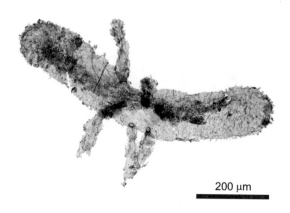

TRILOBITES: THE WORLD THROUGH CRYSTAL EYES
Richard Fortey FGS F.R.S.
Department of Palaeontology, The Natural History Museum, Cromwell Road, London SW7 5BD

Trilobites swarmed in the Palaeozoic seas for nearly 300 million years. They colonised every marine habitat from the shallow shelf to the deep seas, at the same time evolving a variety of form almost unmatched among the invertebrates. They saw the structure of the continents change and change again. They were witnesses to revolutions in the marine ecosystem, and they survived two mass extinctions, only to be laid low by a third. They also afford one of the best examples to show how palaeontological detail can lead to scientific inferences of wide significance.

Trilobites have the oldest visual system preserved in the fossil record which is known in considerable detail: we can - almost literally - see the world through their eyes. Their mineralised calcite lenses are unique in the history of the animal kingdom. They utilised the optical properties of calcite to make images. Some species evolved eyes with thousands of lenses, as many as a dragonfly. Others lost their eyes altogether and were thus the first animals to go blind through choice. The same properties of calcite allow us to reconstruct the visual field of the trilobite. We know that most trilobites looked at the world sideways - but that a few had all round vision. The most specialised eyes were hugely sophisticated, incorporating compensating devices for spherical aberration, for example. So it is possible to have a 'trilobite's eye view' of the Palaeozoic Era.

What would the trilobites have seen? Only rare places where entire fossil faunas are preserved (*Konservat-lagerstatten*) like the Burgess Shale give us a relatively complete picture of the animals that lived alongside them, including a selection of those animals with bodies lacking shells. It is clear, though, that trilobites were only one part of a great early radiation of the jointed-limbed animals, the arthropods, and that their tough, mineralised exoskeletons bias the fossil record in their favour. All our speculations about trilobite 'communities' should bear this in mind - they may well have been part of a far more extensive ecology of which we have only glimpses. However, it is their superb fossil record that allows us to use them as 'experimental material' in a way which is not possible with other arthropods.

A traditional view always had the trilobites as the most primitive arthropods - a view that persisted among zoologists until quite recently. This was largely because they were for a long time the earliest fossil arthropods known. The discovery of rich Lower Cambrian *Konservat lagerstatten* such as those from Greenland and China has made it clear that they do not hold such a privileged position in arthropod evolution. To be sure, their branched (biramous) limbs - which are generally similar along the length of the animal are shared with a whole array of primitive arthropods. But even at this early stage in arthropod evolution trilobites had moved a long way from a basal arthropod groundplan, even without taking into account the advanced characteristics of a calcite dorsal exoskeleton, and unique visual system. Since trilobites were already differentiated into several very different kinds at their first appearance, the writer holds the view that there must have been an earlier phase of intense speciation of which we have (as yet) no fossil record. And since the trilobites have to slot into the greater story of the differentiation of the *whole* of the arthropods this implies a still earlier level of history and the question arises of how far into the Precambrian this extends. An objective attempt to look at these questions involves cladistic analysis of the way the trilobites fit into the evolutionary "tree" of common descent of all the arthropods; this suggests a striking series of structural changes are necessary assuming evolution from a common ancestor with a velvet-worm (*Peripatus*) (these, too, now have quite a prolific fossil record in the Cambrian). This must have taken time - but how much? Opinions differ.

After their initial radiation, trilobites moved into almost every marine habitat: they grazed among stromatolites in the shallows, they crawled upon the deep sea floor, where lived many, but by no means all, of the blind species. This habitat preference gives the palaeontologist an excellent way to understand the configuration of ancient ocean margins. Trilobite "communities" were found in a series broadly related to water depth which go along with other factors like oxygen-levels and temperature. Quite soon in the Cambrian, different families of trilobites tended to dominate in onshore and offshore sites. Shallow-to-deep-water profiles have been drawn for almost all the subsequent history of the trilobites. Furthermore, because the continents through much of the earlier Palaeozoic were separated widely by oceanic tracts, just as they are today, their trilobite faunas - especially the inshore ones, took different evolutionary paths. In the early Ordovician some families were only found on the North American (Laurentian) continent, while their contemporaries in North Africa and the rest of western Gondwana were completely different. Thus it becomes possible to "read' trilobite faunas as maps of past continents. Laurentia and Gondwana must have been separated by an ocean in the early Ordovician. Baltica was a third, and separate, continent. This kind of information runs in tandem with palaeomagnetic evidence, of course, and the palaeontology and the 'black boxes' don't always agree. But in cases where there has been conflict the maps drawn by trilobites have ultimately been vindicated. Deep water trilobite faunas occur along the margins of former continents; nowadays, they are found in little "pockets" where the rocks that contain them have escaped subsequent subduction. From time to time, such faunas take a jump on to the shelf at periods when marine transgressions especially those induced by global sea-level rises, shift the exterior depth zones into formerly shallow environments. In this way the relative sea-level curves can be reconstructed, a palaeontological test of the onlap-offlap curves constructed by sequence stratigraphers. Fossils in general provide a marvellous independent way of testing theories provided by other branches of Earth Science. Trilobites, you might say, see through a sloppily constructed hypothesis. By the time of the complete assembly of the supercontinent Pangaea the trilobites had died out. But they had survived two (some would say, three) previous periods of mass extinction. One has been claimed in the late

Cambrian, and again at the Cambrian-Ordovician boundary. Certainly there is a big 'turnover' at this time. My view is that much of this 'extinction' is rather due to an accelerated bout of *evolution* causing 'ancestors' to disappear and be replaced by modified descendants. However, there is not much question that the end of the Ordovician was a major trauma for trilobites. Many of the families which had been around since the Cambrian disappeared then: the large, smooth asaphids, the blind agnostids, the delightful trinucleids among them.

This extinction also saw the demise of the writer's favourite trilobites: the pelagic ones. These were animals with all-round vision that swam way above the sea floor on which their fellows lived. Some had eyes fused together into one enormous organ; they probably occupied different depth zones: we can show that some favoured dim light. We have shown by experiment that some were well-streamlined, but the majority were probably relatively sluggish. In some fossil localities near sites of oceanic upwelling they were prodigiously abundant - and one individual species, *Carolinites genacinaca*, is globally distributed. We are used to graptolites with such a distribution, but trilobites are usually far more parochial. The latest Ordovician was associated with a great glaciation, and it is oceanographic changes associated with this event which is usually fingered as the cause of the mass extinction. Sadly, I know of no later trilobite that took to a life in the open ocean. Unlike the benthic forms this habitat was closed to them. The Frasnian - Famennian was the last of a series of Devonian oceanic crises that brought to end a variety of spectacular families with a prior hundred-million year history. These included the spiny trilobites that have become familiar from Moroccan collections: odontopleurids and lichids. Proetida alone survived into the Carboniferous, but they once more radiated into a variety of ecological niches until dwindling to ultimate extinction in the Permian.

This leads us to wonder what were the niches that could support so many different kinds of trilobites. Even allowing for them occupying several depth zones, it is still the case that numerous trilobites could share a single habitat - they must have had several 'trades'. I believe that they were capable of most of the same feeding habits as are living marine arthropods.

Phylogenetic arguments lead to us to conclude that the primitive life mode for the groups was as a predator or a scavenger. This is consistent with the interpretation of the limbs of the Burgess Shale trilobite *Olenoides*. In the absence of many trilobites with preserved limbs interpretation of life habits depends particularly on the structures associated with the plate just in front of the mouth - the hypostome. Trilobites that retained the predatory habit developed a strongly attached or buttressed hypostome, the posterior margin of which often became modified into a fork or grinding surface. It is envisioned that the trilobite ground and manipulated its prey against such surfaces. Not surprisingly, given the calorific value of such food, these trilobites includes the giants of their kind, of which *Paradoxides* may be a familiar example. When seeking prey, they often dug short burrows into the sediment.

Abundant, but smaller trilobites often had the hypostome detached from the rest of the exoskeleton: it lay loosely supported by the basal membrane. These are thought to have been particle or deposit feeders, which made a modest living extracting edible particles from the sediment itself. They may even have been able to use the hypostome as a kind of scoop. The tracks that they left by ploughing through the sediment are characteristic grooves called *Cruziana semiplicata*. They did not grow as large as the predatory forms, and several species became blind. The little trilobite which is on sale in gift-shops, *Elrathia kingi*, from the Cambrian of the western USA, is an example of this kind of trilobite.

A third manner of feeding involved bringing sediment into suspension, and sorting out the edible particles inside a chamber underneath the head. In these forms the hypostome was held up under the head, well above the sediment surface. These trilobites are recognisable by their very convex headshields (compared with the thorax), which are often prolonged into great genal spines. Harpids and trinucleids are familiar examples. They produced rather typical bean-shaped traces.

Within a given feeding mode trilobites might specialise for particle or prey size. Thus two or three animals with the same basic feeding mode could exist side by side. In the Cambrian and Ordovician we can add pelagic trilobites into the ecosystem. This goes some way towards our understanding how so many trilobites could co-exist as we find them in the fossil record. But there are many problems remaining. My own attempts to explain the remarkable trinucleid 'fringe' as an aid to filter feeding is a case in point - I was probably wrong in believing it could allow for egress of feeding currents. However, the solution of these problems is not merely to provide a fascinating footnote to history: they are likely to prove relevant once more to the larger questions about how the Palaeozoic world was constructed, and how its ecology functioned.

THE GREEN REVOLUTION

Dianne Edwards CBE F.R.S.

Department of Earth Sciences, Cardiff University, PO Box 914, Park Place Cardiff CF1 3YE

The colonisation of land by plants - the greening of subaerial surfaces on Earth - was not just a landmark event in the history of life on the planet that involved the origins and diversification of new major plant groups, it was truly a revolution in its impact on terrestrial organisms and on the physical environment. This lecture will document the nature of the plant participants. It will touch on the development of terrestrial ecosystems including soils, fungi, microbes and new animals, on changes in the composition of the atmosphere resulting from increased chemical weathering of rocks and even on changes in the courses of rivers.

Forty years ago, the invasion of the land by plants was considered an almost instantaneous event, marked by the appearance of vascular plants close to the Silurian-Devonian boundary some 400 million years ago. Today, as flowering plants, and to a lesser extent conifers, these vascular plants dominate land vegetation. The earliest representatives were more closely related to the ferns, horsetails and clubmosses (lycophytes) that later formed the bulk of the Carboniferous Coal Measure swamp forests. The most easily recognised of the pioneering colonizers were the lycophytes with their spine-like leaves and low herbaceous habit - a spectacular contrast to the descendent giant Carboniferous arborescent lepidodendrids. These first lycophytes lived alongside plants which were essentially collections of green twigs. They cannot be directly related to any living forms, but from them evolved the horsetails, ferns and ultimately seed plants later in the Devonian. However, in such nondescript twiggy 'axial' fossils, extraordinary preservation of cells preserved by silica, calcium carbonate and iron sulphide reveals that cellular construction and chemistry were virtually identical to the cells in modern plants. Hence the plants themselves must have functioned in a similar way in order to permit survival in the mainly hostile drying terrestrial environments. Thus, the anatomical and biochemical innovations (such as waxy cuticle, stomata, lignified water-conducting cells) evolved in such simple early land plants a few centimetres high that permitted the conquest of the land, remain essential to the functioning and survival of present-day giant redwoods, the tallest inhabitants of our planet.

Early vascular plant fossils are found in Silurian rocks from all over the world, although their early radiations are best recorded in the Old Red Sandstone continent that straddled the palaeoequator some 400 million years ago with Britain on its southern shores. There are, however, clues in the form of spores, broadly similar to the dispersal units found in the earliest vascular plants, that higher plants grew on land some 60 million years earlier in the early part of the Ordovician. No Ordovician body fossils have yet been found and the reconstruction of the plants that produced them and elucidation of their affinities remains one of the major palaeobotanical challenges of the 21st century. The repeated configuration of the spores in ferns and their ultrastructure suggest relationships with mosses and liverworts. Present-day examples lack much of the tissue organisation and chemistry of vascular plants, and are far more prone to degradation. This low fossilisation potential is said to explain the lack of body fossils. A land vegetation composed of moss- and liverwort-like plants would have had the appearance of modern moss "forests" or "turfs". It probably would have been found on any damp and stable surfaces in Ordovician and early Silurian times - surfaces that prior to then would have been coated with a green, or even multi-coloured, crust or slime of bacteria and algae.

These successive waves of ground cover resulted in the build-up of soils with an ever increasing component of organic matter as the standing vegetation became more luxuriant and was subsequently broken down to form humus by fungi and bacteria. The primitive soils proved excellent hunting grounds for the earliest carnivores that included spider-like creatures (trigonotarbids) and centipedes, and for a host of detritus and fungi eating mites and springtails. Fossils of these terrestrial arthropods occur with the earliest land plants. The carbon dioxide produced by the activities of all the decomposers passed, not back into the atmosphere, but became dissolved in water to form weak acids. These leached into the rock substrate and on reacting with the rock, the carbon dioxide became trapped into carbonates. Such chemical processes became more efficient as the sediments were penetrated and disrupted by more and more plant roots, the evolution of which can be traced throughout the Devonian when increasingly large shrubs and eventually trees appeared. The locking up of the carbon dioxide, first removed from the atmosphere by photosynthesising plants, following chemical weathering of rocks is at the heart of models showing major decreases in atmospheric carbon-dioxide concentration through the Palaeozoic. Thus the estimated ten to fifteen times current atmospheric levels in the Ordovician fell to almost current levels by the end of the Devonian. In current popular jargon this meant a change from a greenhouse world in the early Palaeozoic to an ice-house one in the Carboniferous, when there were indeed glaciations second only in the Phanerozoic to the ones we are currently experiencing.

And finally, those same rooting systems would have bound together soils, stabilised both river banks and land surfaces during torrential rains, and hence influenced the courses of rivers. The sediment and soil loss seen after flash floods in deforested areas today is a grim reminder of importance of plant cover in this respect. The green revolution was without doubt a momentous event in the history of the planet!

GREAT EXTINCTIONS

Michael J. Benton

Department of Earth Sciences, University of Bristol, Queens Road, Bristol, BS8 1RJ

1. Introduction

There have been many mass extinctions during the history of life, events during which 50% or more of species died out during a relatively short time. Studies of individual mass extinctions show a variety of patterns, with some apparently taking place extremely rapidly, and others over longer periods of time, some restricted geographically, and others worldwide in extent. There is limited evidence for ecologic selectivity during mass extinction times: the only genera at risk are those with restricted geographic ranges. Most research has focused on the Cretaceous-Tertiary (KT) event, 65 million years ago, which marked the end of the dinosaurs and other dominant reptiles, as well as significant marine groups. Uniquely for the KT event there is abundant evidence of one or more major impacts on the Earth, and these must relate to the extinctions. Evidence for impacts of this sort in association with other major mass extinction events is limited, and it is not clear that there was a single driving mechanism that caused all, or even most, mass extinctions following a periodic cycle.

2. Definition

The meaning of the phrase 'mass extinction' is not entirely clear. The events that are commonly called mass extinctions share many features in common, but differ in others. The common features of mass extinctions may be summarised under three headings:

(1) Many species became extinct, perhaps more than 30% of the extant biota;
(2) The extinct forms span a broad range of ecologies, and typically include marine and nonmarine forms, plants and animals, microscopic and large forms;
(3) The extinctions all happened within a short time, and hence relate to a single cause, or cluster of interlinked causes.

None of these factors can be rendered more precisely for a variety of reasons which will be explored below. In a qualitative way, palaeontologists agree that there have been many mass extinctions in the past, and that these varied greatly in magnitude, but attempts have been made to find a more quantitative definition of which extinctions are truly mass extinctions, and which are more localised or ecologically restricted events.

3. Events

Paleontologists agree that there were seven big mass extinction events, and a number of other smaller events. The Late Precambrian event is ill-defined in terms of timing, but such an event clearly occurred about 600 Myr. ago, when earlier metazoan life forms of the Ediacara type disappeared, and the way was cleared for the dramatic radiation of shelly animals at the beginning of the Cambrian.

A series of mass extinctions occurred during the Late Cambrian, perhaps as many as five, which are marked by major changes in trilobite faunas in North America and other parts of the world. Inarticulate brachiopods were also affected. During these events, and just after, animals in the sea became much more diverse, groups such as articulate brachiopods, corals, fishes, gastropods and cephalopods diversified dramatically.

In the Late Ordovician, further substantial turnovers occurred among marine faunas, with extinction of up to 70% of species. All reef-building animals, as well as many families of brachiopods, echinoderms, ostracods, and trilobites died out. These extinctions are associated with evidence for major climatic changes. Tropical-type reefs and their rich faunas lived around the shores of North America and other land masses that lay around the Equator. Southern continents had, however, drifted over the south pole, and a vast phase of glaciation began. The ice spread north in all directions, cooling the southern oceans, locking water into the ice and lowering sea levels globally. Polar faunas moved towards the tropics, and warm-water faunas died out as the whole tropical belt disappeared.

The fourth of the 'big seven' extinctions occurred during the Late Devonian, and this appears to have been a succession of extinction pulses lasting over 10 Myr. in all. The abundant free-swimming cephalopods were decimated, as were the typical armoured fishes of the Devonian. Substantial losses occurred also among rugose and tabulate corals, articulate brachiopods, crinoids, stromatoporoids, ostracods, and trilobites. Causes could be a major cooling phase associated with anoxia on the seabed or massive impacts of extraterrestrial objects.

The largest of all extinction events, the Permo-Triassic (PTr) event, is astonishingly one of the least-known. The dramatic changeover in faunas and floras at this time has long been recognised, and was used to mark the boundary between the Palaeozoic and Mesozoic eras. Most dominant Palaeozoic groups in the sea disappeared, or were much reduced: rugose and tabulate corals, articulate brachiopods, stenolaemate bryozoans, stalked echinoderms, trilobites, and ammonoids. There were also dramatic changes on land, with widespread extinctions among plants, insects, and tetrapods which led, in all cases, to dramatic long-term changes in the dominant replacing forms. Causes seem to have been earthbound, perhaps related to the fusion of continents into the supercontinent Pangea at this time, with associated loss of coastline and shallow seas, global warming, and possible oceanic anoxia.

The Late Triassic events were major, but not so extensive. A marine mass extinction event at the Triassic-Jurassic boundary has long been recognised by the loss of most ammonoids, many families of brachiopods, bivalves, gastropods, and marine reptiles, as well as the final demise of the conodonts. An earlier event, near the beginning of the Late Triassic, also had effects in the sea, with major turnovers among reef faunas, ammonoids, and echinoderms, but it was particularly important on land. There were large-scale changeovers in floras,and many amphibian and reptile groups disappeared, to be followed by the dramatic radiation of the dinosaurs and pterosaurs, as well as the sphenodontids, crocodilians, and mammals. Causes of these events may have been climatic changes associated with the onset of rifting of Pangea and the opening of the Atlantic, together with drift of continents away from the tropical belt.

The Cretaceous-Tertiary (KT) mass extinction is by far the best-known, both to the public, because of the loss of the dinosaurs, but also to researchers, because of the wealth of excellent geologic sections available for study. As well as the dinosaurs, the pterosaurs, plesiosaurs, mosasaurs, ammonites, belemnites, rudist, trigoniid, and inoceramid bivalves, and most foraminifera disappeared. The postulated causes range from long-term climatic change to instantaneous wipeout following a major extraterrestrial impact. These will be reviewed below.

One mass extinction event often ignored, occurring at the present day, may pass the numerical test when it is assessed in the future. There are currently some 5-30 million species on Earth, of which only about 2 million have been described. Rates of species loss are hard to calculate: for birds, it is known that about 1% of all 9000 species have gone extinct since 1600, but some 20% of bird species are endangered, and could disappear in the next century. Global estimates are based on comparisons with palaeontologic examples, from which it is known that background extinction gives a loss of 2-5 families per Myr., rising to 15-20 families per Myr. during mass extinction phases. At present, perhaps several tens of families are being lost per decade, which clearly scales up to a huge mass extinction rate when considered per Myr.

4. Selectivity

The second defining character of mass extinctions (see above) was that they should be ecologically catholic, that there, should be no selectivity. This is a somewhat counter-intuitive proposition, since most biologists might predict that large animals, top carnivores, taxa with narrow ecologic tolerances, and endemic taxa would be highly extinction-prone. Numerous studies by paleontologists, however, have turned up relatively little evidence for selectivity during mass extinctions. The KT event certainly killed the dinosaurs and some other large reptiles, but a full survey shows that a larger number of microscopic planktonic species died out. It is not clear that niche breadth was a strong factor either, since whole clades containing generalists and specialists disappeared at the same time. There is also no apparent bias towards extinction of top carnivores.

The only evidence of selectivity during mass extinctions has been against species with limited geographic ranges. David Jablonski of the University of Chicago surveyed all bivalve and mollusc species and genera of the latest Cretaceous and earliest Tertiary in North America and in Europe, and he found that genera which were geographically restricted were selectively killed off, when compared to taxa with wider species distributions. Defence against extinction would seem to be a species within a genus that occupies as broad a geographic area as possible. Body size and niche seem to be unimportant.

Geographic realm might also be thought to be significant in selectivity during mass extinction events. It has long been suspected that tropical taxa are more extinction-prone than are those with more polar distributions. This idea was based on the observation that some mass extinction events are associated with an episode of cooling. During such a cooling phase, temperate-belt taxa could migrate towards the tropics, tracking their ideal temperature regimes, but the tropical taxa have nowhere to go, and they are squeezed out. Another study by David Raup and David Jablonski, however, has shown no evidence for latitudinal differences in extinction intensities of bivalves during the KT event.

5. Timing

The third defining character of mass extinctions (see above) concerns their timing. It is clearly important to know whether a particular extinction event lasted for 5 Myr. or one year. At present, stratigraphic resolution is often not good enough to resolve time spans between these two extremes. This is the case even for the much-studied KT event, where opposing experts assert that the extinctions all occurred within a time span of one year or 5 Myr. The dispute arises from problems in fossil sampling and from the inadequacy of dating of mass extinction events (problems in stratigraphy). An assertion that the dinosaurs all died out instantaneously 65 million years ago depends on two kinds of evidence: field observations that dinosaur fossils are relatively abundant through the rocks up to a particular point where they disappear, and evidence that the disappearance occurs at the same level worldwide.

Fossil sampling is a key issue. Even if a palaeontologist can prove that dinosaur fossils suddenly disappear from the rock record at a particular horizon, it cannot simply be assumed that the disappearance is the result of extinction; there may have been an environmental change at that point, and the animals moved elsewhere, or there may have been a substantial hiatus in deposition, or depositional processes may have changed in such a way that bones are no longer buried and preserved. Many aspects of taphonomy (modes of burial and preservation of fossils) must be considered, as well as one of the fundamentals of sedimentary geology, that rocks do not equal time. Many thick rock successions are deposited in a short time, as a result of sudden events, such as rock slides, floods, storms, and turbidity flows, whereas other thin parts of a rock sequence may represent vast spans of time. Intensity of study is also important: Ward (1990) showed how his records of ammonite extinction at the KT boundary changed with more field collecting. 'The pattern that he obtained changed from a rather gradual dying off to a more catastrophic demise as the result of more collecting days.

Stratigraphic issues are also crucial. In dating mass extinctions, the first guide is biostratigraphy, the use of fossils to establish relative ages, and to correlate rock units of the same age from continent to continent. The techniques usually work well in defining time bands of 0.5-1 Myr. duration, but are problematic for shorter intervals. Exact age dating using radiometric techniques may give rather precise dates, but the real error may still be too large for biologic purposes. Further, radiometric techniques may only be used on certain rock types, such as volcanic lavas. Other dating techniques have been applied, and may become more precise in the future: at present, they are insufficient to guarantee discrimination between instant events and events that lasted for 1 Myr.

6. Causes

The key question behind all investigation of mass extinctions is, what were the causes? It is impossible to review the multitudes of causes for mass extinctions that have been proposed in the literature, so this commentary will focus on the two that have attracted most attention, the PTr event, 250 Myr. ago, and the KT event, 65 Myr. ago.

The PTr event has been surprisingly little studied, especially in view of the magnitude of the extinctions. The reason for the relative lack of attention may be that some of the best sections across this time interval occur in China and Pakistan, but detailed work is at last being done on these. In his review of current knowledge of the PTr event, Doug Erwin of the Smithsonian Institution, points out that some data suggest that the event may have been drawn out over the whole of the Late Permian, a span of 10 Myr. or more, while others believe that the event was truly rapid. Postulated models for the extinction include the following: (1) the continents were fusing as Pangaea, and this reduced biogeographic realms on land and in the sea; (2) global temperatures increased; (3) global temperatures decreased; (4) salinity of the sea was reduced; (5) major regression of the sea; (6) seas became anoxic; (7) major volcanic eruptions caused poisoning and excess carbon dioxide; (8) major impact caused poisoning! excess carbon dioxide! blacking-out of the Sun and consequent freezing. Erwin rejects global cooling (3), and notes that there is little evidence for salinity reduction (4), volcanic poisoning (7), and impact (8). He prefers to tie the remaining explanations together, and to link them as outcomes of the major late Permian marine regression and of the outpouring of the Siberian volcanic traps, enormous volumes of lavas that were erupted at this time.

Geologists and paleontologists have devoted astonishing efforts to disentangling what happened 65 Myr. ago during the KT event. Some 500-1000 publications come out each year on this subject, and scarcely a week passes without a report in Nature or Science. This intensity of research has been maintained since 1980, when Luis Alvarez of the University of California at Berkeley, and colleagues, published their view that the extinctions had been caused by the impact of a 10km diameter asteroid on the Earth. The impact caused massive extinctions by throwing up a vast dust cloud which blocked out the sun and prevented photosynthesis, and hence plants died off, followed by herbivores, and then carnivores.

There are two key pieces of evidence for the impact hypothesis, an iridium anomaly worldwide at the KT boundary, and associated shocked quartz. Iridium is a platinum-group element that is rare on the Earth's crust, and reaches the Earth from space in meteorites, at a low average rate of accretion. At the KT boundary, that rate increased dramatically, giving an iridium spike. Further, several sections have also yielded shocked quartz, grains of quartz bearing crisscrossing lines produced by the pressure of an impact. Other evidence is geochemical and palaeontological. A catastrophic extinction is indicated by sudden plankton and other marine extinctions in certain section and by abrupt shifts in pollen ratios at some KT boundaries. The shifts in pollen ratios show a sudden loss of angiosperm taxa and their replacement by ferns, and then a progressive return to normal floras. This fern spike, found at many terrestrial KT boundary sections is interpreted as indicating the aftermath of a catastrophic ash fall: ferns recover first and colonise the new surface, followed eventually by the angiosperms after soils begin to develop. This interpretation has been made by analogy with observed floral changes after major volcanic eruptions.

This 'basic' catastrophist model requires that the KT extinction occurred geologically overnight, or at least within a year or so. A variant on this basic model allows for catastrophic extinction in a stepwise manner, involving numerous showers of comets over a span of 1-3 Myr. Such precision of dating may be impossible: the KT boundary may be identified to the nearest millimetre within any single rock section, and it may be confirmed by the disappearance of the last bones of dinosaurs and by pollen changes on land, and by changes in plankton and invertebrate fossils in the sea. However, other techniques are necessary to correlate such disappearances from place to place around the world, and to confirm that they occurred at the same time everywhere.

The main alternative to the extraterrestrial catastrophist explanation for the KT mass extinction is the gradualist model, which sees declines in many groups of organisms caused by long-term climatic changes in which the subtropical lush dinosaurian habitats gave way to the strongly seasonal temperate conifer-dominated mammalian habitats. This gradual ecosystem change model has been challenged on the basis of problems in exact correlation of the isolated mammal faunas. The gradualist scenario has been extended to cover all aspects of the KT events on land and in the sea, with evidence from the gradual declines of many groups through the Late Cretaceous. Climatic changes on land are linked to changes in sea level and in the area of warm shallow-water seas.

Recent evidence of the site of impact has strengthened the catastrophist model for the KT event. A putative crater, the Chicxulub Crater, has been identified deep in Late Cretaceous sediments on the Yucatan peninsula, Central America, and it seems to have produced a range of physical effects in the proximity. A ring of coeval coastline deposits show evidence for tsunami (massive tidal wave) activity, presumably set off by a vast impact into the proto-Caribbean. Further, the KT boundary clays ringing the site also yield abundant shocked quartz and glassy spherules that supposedly match geochemically the bedrock under the crater site. Further afield, the boundary layer is thinner, there are no tsunami deposits, spherules are smaller or absent, and shocked quartz is less abundant.

Another twist to the KT story is that a third school of thought has gained some ground in recent years, the view that most of the KT phenomena may be explained by volcanic activity. The Deccan Traps in India represent a vast outpouring of lava which occurred over the 2-3 Myr. spanning the KT boundary. Supporters of the volcanic model seek to explain all the physical indicators of catastrophe (iridium, shocked quartz, spherules, and the like) and the biologic consequences as the result of the eruption of the Deccan Traps. In some interpretations, the volcanic model explains instantaneous catastrophic extinction, while in others it allows a span of 3 Myr. or so, for a more gradualistic pattern of dying off caused by successive eruption episodes.

Thus, the geochemical and petrological data such as the iridium anomaly, shocked quartz, and glassy spherules, as well as the Chicxulub Crater give strong evidence for a major impact on Earth 65 Myr. ago, although some aspects might also support a volcanic model. Much of the palaeontologic data supports the view of instantaneous extinction, but the majority still indicates longer-term extinction over 1-2 Myr. Key research questions are whether the long-term dying-off is a genuine pattern, or whether it is partly an artifact of incomplete fossil collecting, and, if the impact occurred, how it actually caused the patterns of extinction that occurred. Available killing models are either biologically unlikely, or too catastrophic: recall that a killing scenario must take account of the fact that 75% of families survived the KT event, many of them seemingly entirely unaffected. Whether the two models can be combined so that the long-term declines are explained by gradual changes in sea-level and climate and the final disappearances at the KT boundary were the result of impact-induced stresses is hard to tell.

Further reading

Alvarez, W. and Asaro, F. 1990. An extraterrestrial impact. *Scientific American*, Oct. 1990,44-52. A popular account of the impact hypothesis for the KT mass extinction.

Benton, M. J. 1990. Scientific methodologies in collision; The history of the study of the extinction of the dinosaurs. *Evolutionary Biology, 24*, 37 1-400. A review of the 100 or more theories that have been published to explain the extinction of the dinosaurs, many of them ridiculous, others worthy of further study.

Courtillot, V. E. 1990. A volcanic eruption. *Scientific American*, Oct. 1990, 53-60. A popular account of the volcanic hypothesis for the KT mass extinction.

Erwin, D. H. 1993. The *Great Paleozoic Crisis: Life and Death in the Permian*. Columbia University Press, New York, 327 pp. A detailed account of the Permo-Triassic extinction event, summarizing how much (and how little) is known about the biggest mass extinction of all time.

Hallam, A. and Wignall, P. 1997. *Mass extinctions and their aftermath*. Oxford University Press. The best single-volume text on current views.

Raup, D. M. 1991. *Extinction: bad genes or bad luck*. Norton, New York. An engaging and informed account of the impact model of periodic mass extinctions.

Ryder, G., Fastovsky, D., and Gartner, S. (editors) 1996. The Cretaceous-Tertiary event and other catastrophes in earth history. *Geological Society of America Special Paper, 247*, 1-631. The best review volume, containing 58 papers on all aspects of current research on mass extinctions.

WINNERS AND LOSERS
WHAT CAN WE LEARN OF THE FUTURE FROM THE PAST?

H.S. Torrens
School of Earth Sciences and Geography, Keele University, ST 5 5BG.

History	**Science**
"History is the science of what never happens twice"	"Whenever we notice a remarkable effect, our first question ought to be, can it be reproduced"
Paul Valery	John Herschel

1. Introduction

As the quotations above make crystal clear, the accurate ("scientific") answer to the question posed in my title is that we can learn "precisely" nothing. But history, despite its continuing 'continental' scale drift away from science, has value in arbitrating the past achievements of geology. It is this process which enables historians (and the few who will listen to them) to proclaim sadly that many of the past sins of geology and of geologists will be promoted well into the (ever more uncertain) future. Some real patterns can be discerned about the past of geology and our treatment of it since (however motivated) and thus allow some, hopefully interesting, lessons for the future to be pointed out.

2) Breakthroughs in Geology

When I asked a random group of geologically inclined people to list what they considered the most significant breakthroughs to have happened in geology over the last two centuries, i.e. since the time when the study of the earth conveniently became a science around 1800, the following evolved (but in no particular order of significance) with names alongside of some of those who were thought to have made major contributions to those breakthroughs.

1) The significance of unconformity - John Strachey, James Hutton, William Smith
2) The significance of glaciation - Louis Agassiz
3) Strata identified by fossils - William Smith
4) The recognition of formerly intrusive and extrusive rocks - James Hutton
5) The application of microscopy to geology - Robert Hooke, Henry Clifton Sorby
6) The revelation of the antiquity of the earth from radioactivity, meteorites & geochemistry - Arthur Holmes
7) The fact of continental drift - Alfred Wegener, Arthur Holmes
8) The use of geophysics in oil prospecting - William Haseman and John Karcher

3. Problem One

The list exposes as many problems as it claims to reveal. First the preponderance is British (simply because I had asked British people for their opinions). Only one is Swiss, one German, and two American. This brings me to the first problem for both science and history; the problem of nationalism, or worse of chauvinism (the scale of that crime being best revealed here by the French word we use to express it). As a non-geological example, study the translated quotation of June 1816 below (and in moments of boredom during the lecture ponder why it is so very vituperative!)

> "The English unite to their talent of appropriating the discoveries of others, the audacity to then pretend to have been their original inventors and they then recommend to those they have so plundered that they should believe them. In this way they have stolen from Pascal his hydraulic pump, from Dalenne his fire engine, gas lighting from Lebon, the naval gun carriage from Montalembert, and from Guyton de Morveau his discoveries in disinfection. One could cite more than 200 such plagiarisms in both the sciences and in the arts. They have even had the nerve to play two pieces by Moliere in their theatres but these they gave not as translations, but as original works!".

For an example of this problem in geology see the English review of a French History of Geology published in 1991. The reviewer concluded that this attempt:

> "to rewrite the history of geology in terms of the work of dozens of obscure Frenchmen... was grotesque" (Nature, vol. 354, pp. 27-8, 1991).

This leads us to the related problem of revisionism. David Landes in a recent 1999 book has memorably characterised the:

> "cyclical revisionism that characterizes all the social sciences. The best way to attract attention, get a PhD., get a good job, get promoted, is to stand [existing} things on their head. As a cynic once put it, we climb on the backs of our predecessors".

This was in supposed contrast to 'the ways of science' where, as Isaac Newton - voted (but only by the British!) together with Charles Darwin as 'the men of the millennium' - had written in 1676, "if he had seen further, it was by standing on the shoulders of giants". One may confidently predict that both chauvinism and revisionism will flourish in the future even more then they have in the past (but note that I write this just as a new beef war is breaking out between the 'snail eating' French and the 'perfidious' English...).

4. Problem Two

The dividing line between revision and revisionism is razor-thin. The recently completed revision of the New Dictionary of National Biography (Oxford University Press, 2004, forthcoming) has revealed some wonderful factual errors for some of the geologists featured in the original edition. My favourites are the 1885 entry for Robert Bakewell (1767-1843 - dates corrected), author of the first adequate textbook of geology in English (many editions English, German and American from 1813 to 1838). This told us that when Bakewell was asked by the Countess of Oxford if he was related to the other Robert Bakewell, the Famous animal breeder, "he replied that there was no relation between them". The original source claims the complete opposite! The entry for Joseph Carne (1782-1858) claimed instead that one of his Cornish geology papers proved so inspirational in far off east Germany that it inspired a visit to Cornwall all the way from Freiberg by Abraham Werner (1749-1817). Sadly any such visit was entirely posthumous.

But the same revision of the NDNB has also revealed how few:

a) non-academic 'practitioners' of geology (people who earned their livings from doing geology)
b) 'amateurs' (a category of particular interest to the Geologists' Association and particularly this member of it, who was inspired to take up geology by some of them)
c) women were included in the original. In this new edition some better attention has been paid to all three categories.

The case of some now included, like the stratigrapher Sydney Savory Buckman (1860-1929), shows how complex the assessment of 'past greats' in geology is. But 1999 has at least been notable for the (?first ever) conference held to honour a woman geologist, Mary Anning (1799-1847) of Lyme Regis. That these three same categories (non - academic professionals, amateurs, women) will hold the same marginalised positions in future geology is another confident prediction we can make. But please let us not maintain the 1992 myth that 'William Smith was able to achieve so much because he never married'! The proven existence, but limited knowledge, of Mrs Mary Ann Smith (1791-1844) now makes her husband's work all the more remarkable.

5. Problem Three

Some of the above 'breakthroughs' took an impossibly long time to qualify for that title, just like The Industrial Revolution, which endless historians have pointed out took so MUCH longer than the political one they had in France. Emigre George Steiner even claimed in 1998 that our lack of any such revolution here proved how....

"this land is blessed with a powerful mediocrity of mind. It has saved you from communism and it has saved you from fascism. You do not care enough about ideas to suffer their consequences".

So, for example, the significance of unconformity noted above, took from 1719 (John Strachey) to 1804 when William Smith first attempted to prospect for coal beneath the same unconformity that Strachey had pointed out before (and probably to) him.

The complexity of the search for whether intrusive rocks were to be recognised in the Earth's crust can be best revealed by reading G.B. Greenough's discussion, as first president of the Geological Society of London, in his Critical Examination of 1819, about whether or not Granite was stratified. If you wanted it to be, you could so easily observe that indeed it was.

Other major 'breakthroughs' were simply rejected at the time they were made. This is famously illustrated by the history of Continental Drift and its rejection as 'impossible' by people like the influential non-mobilist Cambridge geophysicist Harold Jeffreys; a subject and its American dimension which has been wonderfully illuminated by Naomi Oreskes in her recent 1999 book The Rejection of Continental Drift. We might also here recall the April 1963 paper by Lawrence W. Morley, sent to, but rejected by, both Nature and the Journal of Geophysical Research. Historians have since pointed out, despite this, that the 'Vine, Matthews and Morley hypothesis of sea floor spreading' should be called just that. Recall too how the fire in 1978 at Morley's Canadian home, made both Morley's and the historian's case all the more difficult.

6. Some Questions

In the light of all the problems that historians of the earth sciences now face in studying the past, from whatever cause, can we be so sure that we all have 'the truth' so clearly staring us in the face today? Should we be so supportive of the arrogance of RAE [Research Assessment Exercises]? Are we sure that all the Earth Sciences Departments in British Universities which have been recently closed and which will continue to be closed (more prediction!) were all chosen fairly? If one was to claim that RAEs never intended to provide a measure of the quality of research, but only to impose a financial control which bureaucrats wished to impose on British academic geology, would you agree? More crucially for the advance of geology in the future, how would the Jeffreys', Moneys and Huttons have been judged when asked (sorry - told) to partake in these exercises? The French geologist and historian of geology, Francois Ellenberger, noted in 1992 how

"academic bureaucracy was now progressively strangling our profession and inhibiting the freedom of research. Woe unto him who does not submit to a research group, whose scientific programme is assigned by these people who always know better, and who claim to direct the paths of science.
Notably one is forbidden to work in more than one speciality. Today Charles Darwin

would be in serious trouble".

In the face of ever increasingly demanded specialisations, figures with such multi-disciplinary skills and expectations have certainly followed the dinosaurs into extinction.

Yet some exciting fields of geology demand multi-disciplinary skills. I think in particular of Oil Prospecting or the new and exciting field of what we may now call "Impactology". The excitement of this last field in the US is not matched by any such excitement here. One reason may be that we are a more sceptical people as scientists but another is surely that we are much too separate in our specialisms here. The position of geophysics in Britain, whether as part astronomy, part physics or part geology, is certainly not mirrored by its unified position within American science.

Other futures remain as uncertain as ever. Will the role of computers continue to be too dominant in geology? If so, will we be able to see at last on our screens new, and I do hope colourful, cyber-minerals, like Chris Pellant's wonderfully named mineral of 1990 Fryingtonite? Will the vital role of fieldwork (where the real skills of one's geology students could once be instantly tested in the past) continue to decline? Will the history of sequence stratigraphy when it comes to be written prove to be as 'interesting' a topic as I predict (as will also be the history of RAEs)?

7. Some Final Thoughts

The future would be much improved by more humility in our geological science than we have today. If the few historians of geology are so confused about "what actually happened", can we be so sure that geological scientists will not be even more confused (if only because there are so many more of them) about what is so surely "to be known" in the future? Should not the job of future teachers be more to motivate, than merely inform, their students/pupils? Why is no-one yet taking enough notice of existing geological predictions about how soon The Oil will run out? Historians can already tell us how, why and when Coal was 'abandoned'. Might we even dare to hope that when some future Murdoch Media Corporation / BBC want to produce a new geological series like their 1998 Earth Story they will not again claim that

> "Geology used to be so dull that TV producers would only risk making such a programme if there were dinosaurs in it. So... to present this new story of our Earth, the last thing [sic - person!] we wanted was a Geologist"

But I fear they will repeat this and that existing ignorances of public and journalists alike on so many matters geological and on their importance, will continue. I recall the recent idea that a monument to "The Few" of World War Two could be constructed on the Chalk Cliffs of Dover in some "pale blue Dorset granite". We have a lot still to do to explain our unique planet to its inhabitants. When 2097 comes it would be nice to find at last that the British GPO had honoured the Huttons and Lyells of the future on British postage stamps instead of the Enid Blyton ones which instead were used on the stamps of 1997. I can only predict with confidence that neither stamps nor the GPO will have survived. I am equally confident that the history of geology will be of as little interest to future geologists as it is to present ones now. It has always amazed me how little the history of our most historical of sciences interests its present practitioners, and I watch in amazement as even the historical elements within geology (like stratigraphy) get ever more marginalised in favour of the supposedly more important study of geological processes.

THE OCEAN PLANET:
EXCITEMENT AND CHALLENGE OF A NEW FRONTIER

Dorrik A. V. Stow

School of Ocean and Earth Science, Southampton Oceanography Centre
Waterfront Campus, Southampton S014 3ZH

1. Introduction

From the dawn of human history the ocean has served as a hunting ground for fishermen, a highway for coastal ships and, more recently, as a battlefield for our worst excesses. The sheer immensity and unfathomable depths of the oceans have provided endless wonderment for our thinkers, their shoreline a carefree playground for our children, while their incredible beauty and rich vitality have moved us all.

Earth is an ocean planet and the oceans are truly the last great frontier for human endeavour, for scientific discovery and for environmental concern. In many ways, we know less about the deep sea floor than we do about the surface of the moon - we have walked on the surface of our nearest neighbour in space, but we are very far from being able to set foot in the ocean deep. The ocean challenge is now firmly before us and I am certain that, by the end of the next century, our children's children will be as familiar with the current mysteries of the deep seas as we are now with their shoreline.

But it is the environmental challenge that is pre-eminent. Jacques Cousteau, a pioneer of ocean science and its popularisation, once wrote of the oceans that they were:

> *"A threatened oasis. In our solar system, the earth is the only planet with an appreciable supply of liquid water. This rare gift is essential for life and, consequently, as the only intelligent and conscious species, mankind should consider the protection of the water-system - rivers, lakes, seas and oceans - as the first condition for survival."*

The oceans have proved both a barrier to human migration and progress as well as a challenge to our ingenuity. The Asian hordes of hunters and fishermen that first populated the Americas could only walk from Siberia to Alaska when the Bering Strait was dry at the peak of the last Ice Age (some 20,000 years ago), and so onwards down the length of North America, close to ocean for comfort and food, and across the narrow isthmus into an unknown continent beyond. The English Channel has periodically served to separate or unite the British Isles with the rest of Europe, as sea-level has fluctuated. More recently, the vast open waters of the Pacific were the playground of Polynesian explorers, the North Sea and North Atlantic a conquering ground for the Vikings, while the whole world's oceans opened up to the European voyages of discovery through the 15th and early 16th centuries.

The power of the sea to wreak havoc with the ordered lives of people has countless records in the annals of history. The great Minoan civilisation of ancient Crete was brought to its knees by a gigantic wave following a volcanic eruption on Santorini. The most famous Japanese paintings always depict just such a wave or tsunami about to strike the shores of their homeland. Times have changed little in this respect. The earthquake that shook western Turkey and the ensuing tragedy that sent shock waves through the rest of the world early in 1999, had its epicentre beneath the tranquil Aegean Sea. Tropical cyclones can build and intensify at sea to such an extent that, where they cross the shoreline, extremely high winds and heavy rainfall can result in major destruction and widespread flooding. The highly populated coasts of NE India and Bangladesh are always at risk, the former still reeling from a supercyclone that struck in October 1999.

2. Concepts that shape history

For 3000 years at least, philosophers and, later, scientists, have been drawn to the ocean and tinkered at its shore, but only in the last century has the systematic science of oceanography begun to unravel its mysteries. Already these studies have unveiled some of the most momentous discoveries of recent times and led, directly or indirectly, to seminal ideas that shape our thinking of today. These include the realisation that:

- Life on Planet Earth had its humble origins in the primordial ocean some 3.5 billion years ago, and that uncountable legions of animals have lived and perished in the long process of evolution since those first tiny cells stirred; the living world is one of constant evolution and change, of great profusion and profound frailty, of extinction and opportunism.

- The Earth everywhere is in continual motion, albeit at a rate perceptible only in geological time; ocean crust is continually created and destroyed, mountains that rise from the oceans are once again returned as dust to the abyss, before they rise again in their turn.

- Patterns of change are forever cyclic though the timescales vary and the past is never exactly repeated; the cycle of the rocks, of sea-level and of climate are all inextricably linked and closely bound to the oceans and to life.

- The natural environment, which we cohabit with a plethora of other species, is the single most important variable in our survival; many of the natural resources we take from the environment are non-renewable.

These fundamental concepts not only influence the way in which marine scientists look at the sea, but have also reached into daily consciousness. Evolution, motion, cyclicity, change and the environment have an everyday reality beyond ocean science, that helps us to realise our place in the world in its true perspective and significance. An increasingly challenging element of our lives is the preservation and management of the environment and its resources. This strand is closely interwoven into our use and abuse of the oceans.

3. Challenge and change

In the following, I have selected three case studies from my own research to illustrate something of both the scientific challenge and discovery, as well as the environmental challenge and resource issues that face us today.

Highest peak to deepest trough: cycle of the rocks

Some 140 million years ago the Indian subcontinent became detached from the southern supercontinent of Gondwanaland and began a slow northward drift. As the new Indian Ocean opened in its wake so the former Tethys Ocean that once girdled the equatorial world closed before it. Between 60 and 50 million years ago its leading edge, perhaps some form of island arc system, began to collide with the northern landmass of Laurasia. Before long, a full continent-continent collision ensued and a new mountain range began to emerge.

As northward movement was all but impossible, parts of the former ocean crust and its sediment cover, together with the opposing sediment prisms of each continent, were squeezed, folded, buckled and overthrust to form the Earth's highest mountain chain - the Himalaya - now claiming all ten of the world's peaks in excess of 8000 m. But uplift always leads to erosion, so that as the Himalaya mountains continued to grow upwards and outwards over several tens of millions of years, they were progressively denuded by an aggressive regime of weathering and mass wasting.

Working in consort, many of the world's most sediment laden rivers carry this denuded mountain debris principally to the east and south. The Huang He, Chiang Jiang, Mekong and Irrawady rivers all transport enormous loads of suspended sediment to feed the fertile plains and muddy deltas of southeast Asia. The greatest sediment load and second largest water discharge of any river is that of the Ganges-Brahmaputra, building up much of low-lying Bangladesh and the great monsoon wetlands of the Ganges Delta. Ultimately this has led to construction of the world's largest submarine 'delta' - the Bengal Fan - in the NE Indian Ocean.

The Bengal Fan (Figure 1) extends over 3000 km from the delta slope, covers an area in excess of 3 million square kilometres, and is over 16 km thick in its proximal region. In this part, much of the sediment is transferred downslope in gigantic submarine slides and debris flows, far surpassing in size even the largest Himalayan landslides. Some of these slides and flows are transformed by mixing with seawater into turbidity currents, capable of transporting very large volumes of sediment to the extreme distal end of the fan. Sinuous channels that cross the surface of the fan today, having constructed super-highways on the crest of overbank levees, mark the passage of turbidity currents from the recent past.

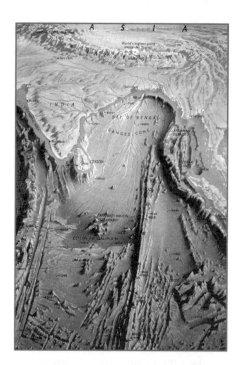

Figure 1 - *Highest peak to deepest trough*. National Geographic Society map of the Indian Ocean floor and neighbouring continent of south and southeast Asia. The Himalayan mountain chain (top) formed from the collision between the Indian and Eurasian plates.

Millions of years of uplift and erosion have led to growth of the mighty Bengal Fan, extending from the delta of the River Ganges to a point south of the equator.

Figure 2 - *Cyprus and the lost Tethys Ocean*. 80 million-year-old ocean crust exposed in this rock formation on the island of Cyprus. The horizontally aligned pillow lavas were once fed molten volcanic basalt via the sub-vertical feeder dykes. The sediments of the deep Tethys Ocean then accumulated above this crust.

Scientific drilling on the distal fan penetrated almost 1000 m of sediments, nearly all of which were deposited as turbidites. Individual beds (from single turbidite events) are as much as 3 m thick, and each may have deposited over an area the size of Sri Lanka. Detailed study of the mineral and chemical composition of these turbidites reveals four different sources: (a) the dominant Himalayan source supplied via the Ganges-Brahmaputra delta; (b) a secondary supply from the Deccan traps volcanic province on the Indian peninsula, via rivers to the eastern coast and thence downslope to the fan; (c) a more minor source of biogenic debris and clays on the warm shallow shelves around Sri Lanka; and (d) small-scale local supply from nearby seamounts. Taken together, these events had a cyclicity of little less than 1000 years, and individually they chart the different evolution of each region. We were able to document, for example, the progressive unroofing of the High Himalaya over the past 18 million years, so that turbidites today contain tracer minerals from the once most deeply buried and chemically unstable mountain core.

Seismic records of the central Indian Ocean below our drill sites show that the whole Indo-Australian plate is under severe compressional stress. The result is a wide region of intraplate deformation in which the ocean crust and overlying sediments are deformed into east-west trending, broad undulations and high-angle thrust faults. The drill record shows that deformation began approximately 7.5 million years ago and has continued intermittently ever since. Heat flow in this area is generally higher than expected for oceanic crust of its age and shows considerable variation. In situ temperature measurements together with chemical analyses of sediment pore waters clearly demonstrate an active hydrothermal circulation system. Deep-sourced hot waters rise up discrete fault planes and then spread out laterally in more permeable silty-sandy layers, leading to localised discharge of warm water onto the deep ocean floor. At the same time, cooler seawater is flowing downwards through underlying permeable silt layers, such that mixing between the two water types occurs.

These are but few of the unique and exciting discoveries made on board the Joides Resolution drillship during one leg of the international Ocean Drilling Program. And just as the sediments that once bordered the north Indian and south Asian landmasses were squeezed and uplifted to form the Himalaya, eroded and carried back down to the ocean deeps, so will begin again the cycle of the rocks. The Bengal Fan itself will be caught-up in a collision of continental plates, and turbidites from the deep sea will form the high peaks of some future mountain chain.

4. Cyprus and the Lost Tethys Ocean

No waters now remain of the Tethys Ocean that closed as Gondwanaland collided with Laurasia, only slithers of rock from its former floors now caught up in the Himalaya, in China and in the Middle East. To marine scientists this is the Lost Ocean of Tethys - a great seaway that extended from Mexico across the middle Atlantic and the Mediterranean into central Asia, reaching its zenith around 150 million years ago. In

Greek mythology, Tethys is a sea-nymph and wife of Oceanus, a mighty river that stretched around the world. Cyprus, alone amongst the Mediterranean islands, was born from this ocean and can therefore tell us something of its long and intriguing history. The story that unfolds is like a picture book of fantastic images telling of a thriving, colourful, changing ocean as every bit alive as the oceans of today.

Mount Olympus, at the very heart of the island and summit of the Troodos Mountains is the legendary home of many gods. To ocean scientists throughout the world, however, it is renowned for quite different reasons. Some 100 million years ago, long before the gods of the ancients, these peaceful slopes were part of the deep-rooted core of a mid-ocean volcano that spewed molten lava onto the sea floor more than 2000 m beneath the ocean surface. Chemical tests on the Cyprus lavas reveal a typical mid-ocean ridge basalt, so that Mount Olympus was once part of the spreading centre from which the Tethys Ocean was born. Through the gradual upwelling of millions upon millions of tons of lava, the Tethys floor grew wider, forcing apart the continents on either side.

When the Tethys had ceased growing, the great continental masses on either side began drifting together. Much of the newly formed ocean crust was forced downwards along ocean trenches where it was partly melted and reabsorbed into the mantle (the layer of earth beneath the outer crust). Some fragments, however, were squeezed upwards in the gigantic collision between the African and Eurasian continents. Troodos is one of these fragments of past ocean floor, known as an ophiolite, forced upwards eventually giving birth to a new island somewhere to the south of the landmass that now includes Turkey.

The Troodos ophiolite is one of the first ever to be recognised for what it was, and it is still one of the few places in the world where you can walk along a roadside and view rocks that sequentially make up the outer crust of the ocean to the deep interior of the Earth's mantle. Thus Cyprus offers scientists the opportunity to study on land the famous "Moho" discontinuity, which marks the base of the Earth's outer crust and which we have been trying for years, unsuccessfully, to drill beneath the ocean floors.

Equally remarkable are other parts of the island where it is possible to walk over acres of rugged basalt lava flows that were once the very floor of the Tethys. We can observe the rounded, pillow-like form (Figure 2) of the basalt that was extruded molten onto the seafloor, the glassy pillow rims from sudden quenching of the hot lava, and millions of tiny holes formed by trapped volcanic gases. In large depressions on the lava surface we can find distinctive brown-coloured metalliferous sediments (known as umbers) formed where hot fluids escaped through the ocean crust, pumping thousands of tons of dissolved iron, manganese and other metals into the cold waters, and great plumes of metal precipitates settled to the seafloor.

Present day examples of these vents, known as black smokers, have only recently been discovered on modern mid-ocean ridges together with a bizarre deep-ocean fauna and flora previously completely unknown to marine biologists. The giant sessile worm-like creatures and delicate algal fronds that have been observed by remotely operated cameras are still largely unstudied because of the hostile conditions in which they exist - temperatures of several hundred degrees, extreme pressures, and highly metal-rich waters. Now, however, scientists can study the fossil remains of such exotic communities in the umbers of Cyprus.

Soon after the volcanic crust was formed as floor to the deep Tethys ocean, the whole area that is now Cyprus was slowly, very slowly covered in a veneer of sediment, a thin blanket that became thicker and thicker as the eons wore on. Spiralling through the sunlit surface waters were billions of tiny creatures that made up the plankton, microscopic plant and animal species different but not dissimilar to those that fill the same ecological niche today. It is their remains, often the most delicate and intricate skeletons made of pure opaline silica or pristine white spar, that accumulate with painstaking slowness over the deep sea floor and, in time harden to form chalk, chert and marl. With powerful electron microscopes we can view even the most minute skeletal fossil and so reconstruct the plankton of that long gone ocean. Rare sharks' teeth are also preserved as testament to a food chain reaching up to the highest order of marine predator.

Nothing lasts forever when viewed in geological time, and so it was that this long period of tranquillity in the great Tethys was due to change. The ocean was closing and already that portion of ocean crust that was to become Cyprus was beginning to push upwards. The rocks demonstrate progressive shallowing of the sea - shelly limestones present a rich diversity of fossil fauna that could only have lived in warm shelf seas and, as the incipient island rose to sealevel, reef-building organisms colonised the substrate. Some of these fossilised reef knolls, fringed by broken talus slopes and encircling quiet lagoonal lime muds, remain almost intact to this day, although they grew and flourished between 10 and 15 million years ago and have now risen several hundred metres above the sea.

There then followed catastrophe for the region and its life, an event so dramatic that its repercussions were felt throughout the world's oceans. For, while Cyprus had been rising, the Tethys Ocean was continuing to close. The Indian subcontinent had already collided with Asia, the Middle East had become sutured together and Africa had nearly closed in on Europe across the Gibraltar Strait, so all that was left of the once mighty Tethys was an irregularly shaped water body roughly similar to the present day Mediterranean and Black Sea. The real trouble started when continued collision in the west finally cut off the Mediterranean from the Atlantic Ocean at about 6.5 million years ago.

The climate at that time was even drier and more arid in the Mediterranean region than it is today so that the influx of river water was unable to keep pace with the rate of evaporation. Progressively the level of the water fell, the rivers that still fed into the remnant basins incised deeply into their banks and cut mighty canyons across the former seafloor. As the water evaporated, the concentration of sea salts increased many times until normal marine life could no longer exist. Salt - tolerant species of red algae survived for longer, but mass death inevitably followed, and still there was no let up in the burning heat. Natural salts began to precipitate from the concentrated brine pools, gypsum being at first most abundant and then, as the seas dried up completely, common rock salt (or halite) lined a gaping, blistering white basin. Life as we know it, indeed life of any kind was unable to exist where once there had been such profusion and diversity.

Complete evaporation of the Mediterranean today would leave a salt deposit about thirty metres thick over the deeper basinal areas, and most of this would be halite. Quite astoundingly there are many hundreds of metres of gypsum preserved on Cyprus as well as on other islands and coastal regions around the Mediterranean, in some cases up to two kilometres thick. Gypsum and halite have also been drilled from beneath the seafloor. Clearly the last remnants of the Tethys Ocean evaporated to dryness or near dryness many times over, being filled from the Atlantic by a tremendous cascade across the Strait of Gibraltar between each episode. This whole process lasted for about half a million years before a more permanent connection was established through the straits.

And so, the turmoil of successive flooding and drying over, a reign of peace and quiet ensued and the Mediterranean slowly gained its present nature and azure calm. Barely a trace was left, save in the rocks, of this most amazing salinity crisis of all time. The Tethys Ocean had finally disappeared forever.

5. Into the abyss - Oil and gas for the 21st century

Twenty five years ago the mining industry was clamouring at the gateway to the deep oceans. Polymetallic (manganese) nodules had been discovered in abundance over many parts of the deep-sea floor. Industry fast developed the technological means for their exploitation, but the bubble burst, metal prices fell and there they lie to this day. The debate then was one of national versus international jurisdiction rather than environmental consequence.

No-one dared consider drilling for oil and gas in such deep waters - after all, the first oil was only just beginning to flow from beneath the relatively shallow waters of the North Sea. But, with such a short life expectancy for these non-renewable energy resources and with further advances in technology, it was not to be long before we again turned to the deep; (Figure 3) this time with unbelievable success! And so the last great wilderness on Earth is now set to define the next generation of oil exploration. In so doing it will also fast-track technological development, challenge scientific understanding, and precipitate environmental change in a region we know less well than the surface of the moon.

Today, indeed, the oil industry is fairly buzzing in this deep, still mysterious realm. New discoveries are more plentiful now than they have been since the early heyday of North Sea oil. Earlier this year, BP-Amoco announced four new discoveries in the Gulf of

Figure 3 - *Into the Abyss.* Scientific drillship JOIDES Resolution exploring below the floors of today's ocean basins. Scientists and the oil industry are now both pushing back this last unexplored frontier on Planet Earth.

Figure 4 - *Environmental challenge.* Peaceful volcanic island and fishing community in the Caribbean. How long can the oceans withstand the pressures of oil exploration and transport, waste disposal and global tourism?

Mexico, including the one billion barrel Crazy Horse field at a water depth of 6000 feet, the largest yet in the deep-water Gulf. Arguably more significant still was their discovery of the Plutonio field in over 4000 feet of water offshore Angola, thus further opening up the deep-water frontiers off West Africa.

These discoveries simply add to a fast growing success story around the world - the Foinhavn and Schiehallion fields west of the Shetland Isles, for example, are now on stream and flowing oil. Petrobras, the Brazilian state oil giant, currently leads the march into deep waters around South America, holding the drilling record at around 8000 feet (2500m) water depth, with further penetration below the seafloor in excess of 12000 feet. Statoil has moved from great success in the North Sea to the deep cold waters west of Norway and farther north towards Svalbard. Extreme high latitude drilling is already meeting with success on the McKenzie Delta slope in the Arctic Ocean, whilst the Oil and Natural Gas Corporation of India is leading the way downslope into the subtropical Indian Ocean.

An estimated 1200 to 1300 oil and gas fields, including discoveries and producing fields, are now known from deep-water turbidite and related systems. The uncertainty in this figure derives from a relative lack of publicly available data from Russia, the former USSR and China. Many of these turbidite fields are from well-established provinces such as California, the North Sea and Gulf of Bohai, that presently lie beneath the continent or below shallow shelf waters. The early giants were almost all from convergent/obliquely convergent margin basins, whereas the later ones are dominantly from divergent margins, including the Gulf of Mexico, Campos, Niger Delta, Lower Congo/Angola, and west of Shetlands. Currently undeveloped giants lie in remote areas of the MacKenzie Delta, the Margarita Basin off Venezuela and on the NW Shelf of Australia.

The discovery and development of all sizes of turbidite fields has shown a sharp increase over the past 20-30 years and the trend looks set to continue. Established provinces with known good source rock capacity are the most favoured basins for future exploration. But additional frontiers include the Baram Delta (NW Borneo), the Mahakam Delta (Kutei), Taranki Basin (offshore New Zealand), the NW Australian margin, and the slopes around the Indian subcontinent and other parts of south and southeast Asia.

The rewards are undoubtedly rich but the stakes are higher than ever before - both economically and environmentally. When a single wildcat exploration well in deep water can cost over £50 million, it is essential to greatly narrow the odds of making that well a discovery, and a large one at that. Where drilling is taking place at the very limits of technical feasibility, there is little margin for error. Where exploration is often into little known or completely virgin parts of the ocean basins, then the environmental consequences must be measured with extreme caution.

6. Environmental challenge

We have experienced an exponential advance in science and technology through the 20th century witnessed, for example, by the space programme. This began with the ambitious dream that the human animal was ready now to explore and conquer outer space, first landing on the moon, later on Mars, and then sending unmanned missions of reconnaissance to the outer planets, Jupiter and Saturn, and out of the solar system beyond. This great project was undoubtedly a crowning achievement for life that had been totally earth-bound for some 3.5 billion years and ocean-bound for the first 3 billion of these. It was also a remarkable luxury when a third of the human race was starving, a further third living in undignified poverty and when 70% had neither adequate medical care nor clean drinking water.

But space exploration brought back a rare and unexpected treasure. Not just the first prized fragments of moon rock and scrapings of dust from the Martian desert nor, important as it was, the knowledge that water and life do not abound on other planets in the solar system but, quite simply, a cosmic view of the earth. For the first time we could truly view the world as a whole, white swirling clouds in the atmosphere, the blue expanse of ocean that covered 70% of its surface. Frontiers between countries for which so many men and women have fought and died through countless years were not visible. We were all passengers on the same small isolated blue planet, third out from the sun. Oceans and continents, mountains and rivers were teaming with a most rare and beautiful life. The Earth and her life systems were one ecological unity.

Ocean space is the last great frontier on this planet. Our scientific and technical capabilities have at last enabled us to begin to penetrate and to know that vast expanse beneath the waves. But they have also brought an ability to radically alter the global ecosystem. At the dawn of a new century we are witnessing major changes to the atmosphere, biosphere and hydrosphere brought about unintentionally by the activities of an ever-increasing human population. Human greed rather than human need views the world as an economic unity - the land has been raped and now we are set to assassinate the oceans. (Figure 4)

As we enter the third millennium, therefore, we face the most important challenge ever - that of careful stewardship and sound management of the planet, not only for ourselves and our children but for the whole rich diversity of life whose world we have the privilege to cohabit.

It is the ocean that seeded this life and that still holds the key to its survival. It is a place that truly encapsulates the enormity of time and the vastness of space, ordered complexity and simple chaos. Now we have only just begun to unravel the endless secrets of the sea and already the new perspectives and insight we have gained are shaping the way we view the world. There is more, so much more to come. As a firm optimist and dedicated marine scientist, I believe that our growing knowledge of how the oceans are entwined in the ecological unity of the Earth, coupled with our new cosmic perspective, will indeed be up to the challenge of the next millennium.

LIVING ON BORROWED TIME - CATASTROPHES TO COME

Bill McGuire FGS

Benfield Greig Hazard Research Centre, University College London,
Gower Street, London WC1E 6BT

1. Introduction

Both the scale and the number of natural disasters are increasing, partly because the world is becoming more overcrowded, and partly because it appears that extreme weather conditions like floods and windstorms are becoming more frequent due to global warming. The cost of natural disasters is also rising dramatically, with economic losses caused by geophysical hazards totalling over ninety billion US dollars in 1998, more than the losses for the whole of the 1960s. Even this impressive figure pales into insignificance, however, when compared with the estimated cost of the first global natural catastrophe. When this happens — and we may not have that long to wait — the cost may not be measured in monetary terms but in the obliteration of all or much of the human race.

Our planet's 4.6 billion-year history has been punctuated by catastrophic events capable of global devastation, but none has occurred in the two thousand years of modern Earth history. This is not surprising, as their frequency is very low. Nevertheless they will happen again and when they do there may well be nowhere to run and nowhere to hide. Three events have the potential to cause major destruction across the planet or at least over a substantial portion thereof. Two of these are terrestrial; a volcanic super-eruption and a giant tsunami caused by the collapse of an oceanic island, and the third — the collision of our planet with an asteroid or comet — has its origin beyond the Earth's atmosphere. The recent Hollywood blockbusters — Deep Impact and Armageddon — have ensured that the impact threat is now familiar to most people and it has even been discussed in the House of Commons. The devastation of which giant tsunami and super-eruptions are capable has, however, gained little publicity to date, although recent geological evidence suggests that their effect on global society could be equally catastrophic.

2. The devastating power of giant tsunami

July 1998 saw one of the worst tsunami disasters in recent years when a submarine earthquake close to the northern coastline of New Guinea generated a series of waves up to seventeen metres high that hammered into fishing villages adjacent to the Sissano lagoon. At least three thousand villagers, many children, died in minutes, either drowned or battered by debris. Such earthquake related - or seismogenic - tsunami are particularly common around the Pacific Rim, and during the twentieth century alone over four hundred tsunami took over fifty thousand lives. Together with impact events and gigantic volcanic eruptions, tsunami have the ability to wreak destruction far from their source. For example, the great Chilean earthquake of 1960 - probably the most powerful quake this century - generated tsunami that killed thousands living on the west coast of South America, but also took lives in Hawaii and in Japan, the latter over fifteen thousand kilometres from the epicentre of the quake. In addition to being able to cause remote destruction, tsunami also travel with incredible speed, perhaps as much as 800 kilometres an hour in deep water. Here they are barely more than a swell a metre or two high, but as they enter the shallower water adjacent to a land mass they can build to heights of tens of metres or more before crashing onto a coastline with the force of an atomic bomb. Although most tsunami are generated by earthquakes, all are not, and in fact some of the most devastating have been caused by volcanic eruptions or landslides. In 1792, part of the Unzen volcano on the Japanese island of Kyushu fell into the sea without warning, generating a number of tsunami that took over fourteen thousand lives in the numerous fishing villages along the coast. Nearly a century later in 1883, the titanic volcanic explosion and collapse of Krakatoa in Indonesia produced tsunami up to forty metres high that scoured the nearby coastlines of Java and Sumatra, killing over thirty-six thousand people.

In recent years, geological evidence has been accumulating that reveals that collapsing volcanic islands have been responsible for some of the greatest tsunami ever known. Around one hundred thousand years ago, for example, a huge chunk of the Big Island of Hawaii - totalling over a thousand cubic kilometres of rock - slid into the Pacific Ocean. The waves generated rode up the flanks of the neighbouring island of Lanai to a height of over three hundred and seventy-five metres, and even when they crashed into the coastline of New South Wales hours later and seven thousand kilometres away they were a terrifying fifteen metres high. A similar event occurring today would devastate the entire Pacific Rim, killing tens of millions and causing damage costing trillions of US dollars. In fact, such collapses appear to occur in the Hawaiian archipelago every twenty thousand to one hundred thousand years. As we don't know when the last one occurred it is difficult to forecast when it might next happen, although we do know that the entire south flank of the active Kilauea volcano on the Big Island is currently sliding seawards —albeit at a few centimetres a year. It is quite possible that the next great volcanic collapse will occur not in the Pacific, but in the Atlantic Basin. In 1949, during the penultimate eruption of the Cumbre Vieja volcano on the Canary Island of La Palma, something like two hundred cubic kilometres of the west flank dropped seaward by about four metres before stopping. This huge rock mass remains unstable and could slide again during the next eruption, this time all the way to the sea. It is more likely, however, that thousands of years will pass before this happens. When it does, however, the great tsunami generated are likely to prove catastrophic for the Caribbean and the eastern seaboard of the United States.

3. Super-eruptions and volcanic winter

Volcanic eruptions range from the quiet emission of lava to gigantic explosions that eject thousands of cubic kilometres of debris. A scale known as the Volcano Explosivity Index or VEI describes the violence of volcanic eruptions. This open-ended index runs from 0 for the most peaceful effusion of lava to 8 for the most cataclysmic of explosive blasts. The scale is logarithmic so each point indicates an eruption ten times more powerful than that immediately below. The famous 1980 eruption of Mount St. Helens (Washington State, USA) registered a 5 on the VEI, while the 1991 blast of Pinatubo (Philippines) scored a 6. We have to go back to the time of the Napoleonic Wars and the eruption of Tambora (Indonesia) in 1815 for the last VEI 7 and to the start of the last ice age over seventy thousand years ago for the most recent 8. This cataclysmic explosion also occurred in Indonesia, at a place called Toba in Sumatra, and appears not only to have devastated the surrounding region but also severely affected the global climate. Due to the logarithmic nature of the VEI scale, the Toba blast had the power of ten Tamboras or a thousand Mount St Helens eruptions, but its terrible impact on the planet was far, far greater. It is difficult to visualise the scale of one of these VEI 8 events, or super-eruptions as they are now known, but something of their devastating power can be gleaned by studying the deposits they leave behind. At Yellowstone in the US State of Wyoming, three super-eruptions have occurred over the last two million years, each time wreaking havoc across North America. The first of these cataclysmic blasts ejected over two thousand cubic kilometres of debris, which was carried over sixteen states. Ash fell as far afield as Des Moines in Iowa, and El Paso in Texas, and even reached the location of Los Angeles in California. Fifteen hundred kilometres from the eruption site, ash lay over a quarter of a metre deep, suffocating plant and animal life. If anything, the Toba blast was even bigger. Here, nearly three thousand cubic kilometres of debris was ejected, much of it high into the stratosphere, along with five thousand million tonnes of sulphuric acid aerosols. Within weeks this material shrouded the entire planet, dramatically reducing the amount of solar radiation and plunging the Earth into a volcanic winter. In places temperatures may have fallen by as much as fifteen degrees Celsius and the northern hemisphere appears to have experienced an average cooling of up to five degrees Celsius. At the time of Toba the Earth was already suffering a fall in temperatures, and it is quite possible that the eruption proved to be the final trigger that plunged the planet into full ice age conditions. There is also new evidence that the Toba blast almost finished off the human race. Recent studies of the variability of human DNA, undertaken at the University of Utah, reveal that it is much less than might be expected given the age of our race. The only explanation appears to be that the DNA found in all humans alive today is descended from that in only three to four thousand individuals living around 70,000 years ago. This dramatic 'bottleneck' in the numbers of our distant ancestors might well be explained by the devastating impact on the race of the Toba super-eruption.

Over the past two million years, it seems that on average, two super-eruptions have occurred every hundred millennia. Given that the Toba blast was around 73,000 years ago it may be time to start worrying about the next cataclysmic eruption and its likely impact on modern society. It is highly probable that the next super-eruption will — at the very least — lead to the loss of at least one growing season worldwide, and consequent mass starvation that could take hundreds of millions of lives. The social and economic impact of a volcanic winter will also be profound, and it is questionable whether our closely interwoven global society would survive.

4. The threat from space

One of the biggest scientific events of the last decade of the last millennium was undoubtedly the collision of the fragments of Comet Shoemaker-Levy with the planet Jupiter. The dramatic images of the impacts focused attention on the threat facing our own planet from space debris, and led to two major films and a deluge of books on the subject. More significantly, the collision ensured that both scientists and governments at last took the impact threat more seriously. This change of perspective was additionally furthered by the unequivocal identification of the impact site of the comet that wiped out the dinosaurs sixty-five million years ago - at Chicxulub off the east coast of Mexico - and improved understanding of the devastating ramifications for the planet. We are now much more aware that space is far from empty. As the Earth travels about the Sun, its orbit intersects the paths of perhaps a billion rock fragments in excess of ten metres across, and maybe a million more with diameters of a hundred metres or more. Objects in this size range can be locally devastating if they collide with the Earth, having the potential to wipe out a major city or a small country. Three times this century - in 1908 (Siberia), 1931 (Brazil), and 1997 (Greenland) - chunks of rock or ice around forty to fifty metres across have made it through the Earth's atmosphere to explode on or just above the surface. Fortunately all three impacts occurred in remote parts of the planet, resulting in little or no loss of life and no damage to man-made structures.

Of much greater concern are larger bodies of rock or ice, in excess of one kilometre across, which have the potential to wipe out a quarter or more of the planet's population, and which are thought to hit the Earth — on average — about once every hundred thousand years or so. Estimates for the numbers of asteroids in this size range whose orbits intersect that of the Earth's range between two and four thousand. Unfortunately, however, the orbital characteristics of only a few hundred have so far been determined, with the balance constituting an unknown and disturbing threat to the survival of modern society. In an attempt to find out more about the positions of these larger bodies, telescopic sky searches are now underway in a number of countries around the world - coordinated by the Spacewatch organisation established by concerned scientists in 1989. As is often the case with what some regard as rather esoteric science, however, the level of funding is inadequate. At the current rate of progress it may take another thousand years before all the Earth-crossing asteroids of one kilometre diameter and greater are located, and by this time it might be too late. Wherever a one- kilometre object hits the Earth, none of the planet would escape its devastating effects. If the object impacted in the ocean, the resulting tsunami would dwarf those produced by a collapsing volcanic island, causing basin-wide ruin and enormous loss of life. The gigantic volume of debris ejected into the stratosphere would, as in the case of a super-eruption dramatically reduce solar radiation reaching the surface, and a cosmic winter would follow. The total death toll is likely to be in excess of a billion and it is questionable whether our global society could survive.

5. Is there anything we can do?

One thing we can be certain of is that a global natural catastrophe will occur at some time in the future. The problem is that because modern society has never experienced anything on this scale, a failure of imagination becomes apparent when confronting government officials, disaster managers, insurance companies, and others in the 'disaster business'. Before anything can be done, it is essential to get the message across that an impact, a super-eruption, or a giant tsunami will happen again, perhaps many thousands of years hence, but perhaps tomorrow. Once, as a society, we face this fact, we have already made a start on the long road towards coping with the devastating effects of these global catastrophes. During the Cold War, the terrible fear of an all-out nuclear exchange resulted in many countries developing civil defence plans to cope - as much as could be expected - with the appalling consequences of such a scenario. Equipped with our new knowledge of global natural catastrophes and their devastating legacies, it is to be hoped now that similar attention and effort can be paid to ensuring that appropriate measures are in place to minimise - as far as is feasible - the effects of a cosmic or volcanic winter, as opposed to a nuclear one.

Further reading

Apocalypse! A natural history of Global Disasters
Bill McGuire 1999 Cassell. £14.99 paperback. ISBN 0-304-35209-8

LIVING WITH VOLCANIC RISK

Hazel Rymer

Department of Earth Sciences,
The Open University, Walton Hall, Milton Keynes, Bucks, MK7 6AA

Abstract

The 1990s were designated the International Decade of Natural Disaster Reduction (IDNDR) by the United Nations and considerable research effort has gone into achieving a better understanding of volcanic processes and public understanding of volcanic phenomena. Some eruptions have been predicted successfully and thousands of lives have been saved through evacuation and well co-ordinated aid programs. The IDNDR followed hard on the heels of the 1985 disaster at Nevado del Ruiz in Columbia where more than 22,0000 people died in one night following a small eruption and a large mudslide. It seemed obvious that a better understanding of the workings of active volcanoes and increased public awareness could dramatically reduce the human cost of natural disasters. To some extent this view seems to have been correct, as a much larger eruption, at Pinatubo in the Philippines in 1991, is considered to have been a success from the point of view of prediction and evacuation. There is evidence though, that the education of the public, the local political and economic situation still play an important role in determining whether a disaster is averted or not. Famous historical eruptions have captured the public imagination. Hollywood films use dramatic special effects to glamorise volcanology and to some extent educate audiences. The historic eruptions of Vesuvius (destroying Pompeii in AD79) and Krakatoa (killing more than 36,000 in 1883) are well known to us through books and films, but many ancient civilisations also had stories and myths relating to volcanoes and volcanic events. There are lessons that can be learnt from past major eruptions and their effects on the local population or on civilisation in general; the interdependence of the global economy with most nations of the world now means that a major eruption can have significant global economic consequences.

1. Volcanic hazards

The risk that a community is exposed to from a volcanic hazard depends on its vulnerability and this may be expressed by the relationship

$$\text{Risk} = \text{hazard} \times \text{vulnerability}$$

The hazard may be ash fall, pyroclastic flows, lava flows, lahars, gas, tsunami or some combination of these. The hazard depends on the type of volcano, the time since the last eruption of that volcano, the geographical location, the local climate and the time of year. The location and timing of a volcanic event affects the risk since wind directions and strengths in the upper atmosphere vary with latitude and season. This means that an ash eruption might be transported around the globe at one time, but would remain confined to a small region at another time.

Vulnerability is a measure of the number of people in the affected area and the local infrastructure (which includes housing, communications, transport etc.). It is obvious that the risk increases with the number of people living near a volcano, but it also depends on the type of eruption (and therefore the hazard). As the global population increases, the risk of a volcanic disaster increases simply because more and more people live near active volcanoes. However, increasing globalisation reduces the vulnerability of communities by raising their awareness of potential hazards and levels of preparedness.

As the world population continues to grow and the complexity of life increases, the vulnerability of communities to natural disaster increases, but so too does the ability to mitigate disaster. It is interesting to note how the distribution of causes of death in volcanic eruptions has varied throughout recorded history (Table 1), although there are considerable uncertainties in some of the older data.

Table 1

Cause of Death	1600-1899	1900-1986	1987-1994
Direct	38400	68300	395
Starvation	61100	3200	600
Tsunami	40600	400	-
Gas	-	1900	6
Other	15100	2200	33
Total	*155200*	*76000*	*1034*
Average per year	**5200**	**880**	**130**

Data from Simkin and Siebert, (1994), Tilling (1989) and Tanguy et al. (1998).

The statistics are dominated by a few large events; the 1783 eruption of Lakagigar, the 1815 eruption of Tambora, the 1883 eruption of Krakatoa, the 1902 eruption of Pelee and the 1985 eruption of Nevado del Ruiz. Nevertheless, it is significant that the average number of deaths per year caused directly by eruptions (e.g. deaths in pyroclastic flows and lahars etc.) rose dramatically from 130 between 1600 and 1899 to 730 in the twentieth century. The number of direct deaths is to some extent a consequence of increased population, but may also reflect better reporting of events. Certainly the number of deaths caused by volcanic events prior to the 1600s outside Europe would be very difficult to quantify and substantiate now. One positive consequence of increasing globalisation and communication is that aid in the form of emergency shelters, food and vaccines is now readily available to survivors of volcanic disasters resulting in fewer post-eruption deaths due to starvation and disease. The annual death rate from these causes has fallen from over 200 between 1600 and 1899 to 40 in the twentieth century.

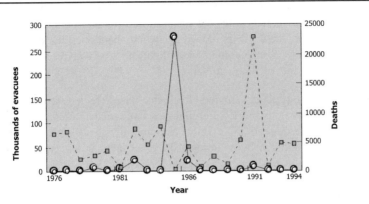

Figure 1 - The number of people evacuated (squares) during volcanic crises has remained surprisingly constant in recent years, although the Pinatubo eruption in 1991 is a clear anomaly. Increasingly good volcano surveillance and communication between scientists, the media and public have ensured that the numbers evacuated are proportional to the risk and that the number of deaths (circles) continues to fall.

2. Past eruptions

The Bronze Age eruption of Thera (also known as Santorini) some 70 km north of Crete coincided with the demise of the Minoan civilisation. The tsunami caused by the caldera collapse would have flooded the eastern Mediterranean shoreline and ash from the eruption reached as far as the Nile delta. The memory of these events may have given rise to stories in the Bible and Greek Mythology of great floods, darkness in all the land and the lost continent of Atlantis. There were earthquakes and small eruptions that served as precursors to the devastating eruption in about 1620 BC and although towns were buried in ash, the lack of buried bodies found in excavations suggests that many people moved away before the climactic event. Whether they were previously weakened by a series of devastating earthquakes, or subsequently as a result of the eruption is uncertain, but the Minoan influence in the Mediterranean declined rapidly in the seventeenth century BC. This is an early example of the political and economic disruption that a major volcanic eruption can cause.

In 79 AD Vesuvius erupted violently and thousands of people died when the prosperous Roman towns of Pompeii and Herculaneum were covered in almost 3m of ash. Precursory earthquakes and small eruptions were not recognised at the time as a warning. Even the appearance of a column of ash reaching several km up from the summit of Vesuvius would have been considered an interesting phenomenon by most people rather than the beginning of a momentous eruption. The towns were too deeply buried to reuse immediately after the eruption and fields around the town would also have been unusable, so survivors moved away and abandoned the devastated area. The location of the towns was forgotten. Much later the area was resettled and millions of people now live in this region near Naples.

The first eruption to produce climatic effects that people recognised at the time as being caused by a volcano, was the 1783 eruption of Lakagigar in Iceland. About 14 km3 of basaltic tephra were erupted in 8 months. Although it was not such a violent eruption as those at Tambora and Krakatoa almost 100 years later, it was a relatively long-lived eruption. A dense bluish acidic haze covered Iceland and large quantities of SO_2, HF and HCl were also emitted and rained out onto the land; 75% of the livestock and 25% of the human population of Iceland died as a result of starvation and ingestion of lethal amounts of fluorine. Acid rain also fell in Scotland and Scandinavia and the acidic smog drifted over Europe lowering the temperature by 1°C and producing the coldest winter in New Jersey, USA in 225 years.

The largest historical eruption, that of Tambora (Indonesia) in 1815, is unfortunately one of the least well documented. Over 50 km3 of trachyandesite was erupted and the column reached an altitude of 43 km. Pyroclastic flows killed 11,000 people, but a further 50,000 later died of famine (Tanguy et al. 1998). Rainfall was unusually high in northern Europe the following summer and the temperatures were about 0.5°C lower than normal. The year became known in Europe as 'The year without a summer'.

In 1883, the famous eruption of Krakatoa produced pyroclastic flows that killed 4-5,000 people and tsunamis that killed 32,000 people. Again there were precursors to the eruption, but they would not have been recognised as such at the time. About 20 km3 of dacitic magma were erupted during the climactic phase of this event and the plinian column rose over 40 km. The explosion was heard almost 5000 km away and pressure waves from the eruption were detectable right around the world. The tsunami travelled around the Sundra Straits and swept away many coastal towns and villages. Northern hemisphere temperatures were 0.25°C cooler than average for 2 years following the eruption.

Widespread hardship due to crop failures and the spread of disease in weakened populations followed these eruptions. Modern global communications and greater prosperity however do not mean that such disasters are restricted to history. The twentieth century has also witnessed huge volcanic disasters, and the increasingly dense population means that even relatively small eruptions can produce alarming deathtolls. It has been estimated that some 350-500 million people now live in active volcanic regions (Tanguy et al. 1998).

3. Some eruptions of the twentieth century

On 8th May 1902, the beautiful Caribbean island of Martinique was disrupted by lahars and pyroclastic flows from Mt Pelee. Precursors to the fatal eruption were seen and felt for a few weeks and hundreds of people left the town, but many hundreds more moved in from the surrounding rural areas. Volcanic eruptions were well known by 1902 and Mt Pelee had erupted in living memory. Nevertheless for most people, it seemed better to stay in the prosperous town than to leave property and possessions and move away. Economics plays a role here, but even some of those who could easily afford to leave by boat chose not to because they did not believe that the eruption was significant. Local politics were important here also as elections were due to be held on May 11th. No plans for evacuation were made. A pyroclastic flow killed over 27,000 people in just a few minutes on May 8th The eruption persisted for several months and a further 2,000 were killed when another flow went in a different direction and covered a village that had been unaffected by the earlier activity.

It really began to look as though a similar tragedy could never happen again — better education and communication should mean that volcanic disasters are a relic of the past. On May 18th 1980, Mount St. Helens volcano in Washington State, USA erupted 0.1 km3 of andesitic magma. It had been closely monitored and as the eruption approached, the accuracy of the forecasts improved. Hazard maps (to identify locations expected to be affected by particular hazards) had already been drawn up and a substantial evacuation zone defined. The 60 people who died were all within the evacuation area. Thousands would have died at this popular tourist location if the warnings had not been heeded.

The small (0.01 km3) eruption on 13th November in 1985 at Nevado del Ruiz in Colombia should never have resulted in the death of more than 22,000 people at Armero. Especially poignant, is the fact that the volcano was known to be active, and an international team of scientists had visited the area, drawn up a hazard map and warned the authorities of the possibility of a small eruption producing a lahar that would destroy towns such as Armero. Indeed the town was built on the deposits of earlier lahars. Ancient traditions in the area told of mudflows, but still the tragedy happened. An evacuation order was issued but it was not received in time. The local population had not been informed of the situation and no evacuation took place.

Pinatubo in the Philippines erupted on 13th June 1991 after 2 months of precursory activity. The volcano was well monitored and hazard maps had been drawn up. In all about 250,000 people were evacuated, including military personnel and their dependents at the nearby US Clark Air Base. Several hundred people died during and immediately after the eruption, mainly due to mudflows following a typhoon and disease in the refugee camps. This eruption is often used as an example of the success of modern volcanology; it is certainly true that the eruption forecasting was good and, crucially communication between scientists, officials and the population was excellent. The US

Air Base that had existed since the beginning of the century was closed after the eruption however, and handed back to the Philippine government with the loss of thousands of Philippine jobs. It was considered too hazardous and expensive a location for the US to maintain a presence there. Global climate change has become a topic of public concern and political debate in recent years and the effects of the Pinatubo eruption were closely monitored. Global temperatures were depressed by a fraction of a degree in the years after the eruption to some extent mitigating global warming at the time. However, the interaction of the volcanic plume with man made chloro-flouro aerosols was found to be extremely damaging to the ozone layer.

Closer to home, Mount Etna on Sicily, has been almost continuously active in historic times. The eruption in 1991-1993 is important because lava was erupted at a relatively high rate (about 10 m3 s-1) from a flank fissure into a valley and towards the large and prosperous town of Zafferana Etnea. There was no direct threat to life, as the basaltic lava moved slower than walking pace, but several attempts were made to divert the flow because of the economic consequences of disruption to the town. Although a pyroclastic flow is more devastating, even a slow moving lava flow will cause chaos when it enters a town. It blocks roads, sets fire to and knocks down buildings. The electricity supply, water supply and all other services will be disrupted. A power cut lasting only a few minutes in a large city has serious consequences in hospitals, schools and other community buildings. If disruption lasts for days, weeks or even longer, the effects are likely to be fatal. Individuals may lose property and revenue; insurance companies and the government may lose very substantial sums. The Etnean lava flow was successfully diverted in 1992, but the cost was several million pounds. The cost of not succeeding would have been higher still. Hundreds of businesses might have become bankrupted; the town of Zafferana Etnea would not function properly until rebuilding and salvage operations could get underway.

The British dependency of Montserrat has hit the headlines during the last few years as pyroclastic flows claimed lives and destroyed the capital city, the airport and much of this beautiful Caribbean island. Most of the population has left the island and those who are left are living in the northern region, away from the volcano in the south. The eruptions were predicted and the deaths occurred within the evacuated area, but the political fallout of the whole event looks set to outlast the eruption.

4. Volcano monitoring

Volcano monitoring at its most effective is a synergy between basic science and hazard assessment. Techniques can be divided into 2 types; satellite based and ground based, and both can be further sub-divided into active and passive techniques.

Satellite based techniques are proliferating and producing more data than can be handled at present. Satellites in stable orbits can either stay over the same part of the Earth (geo-stationary orbit) or move relative to the Earth's surface. The repeat period at which a satellite views the same part of the Earth's surface ranges from a few hours to many months depending on the type of orbit. Sensors on board satellites can either passively measure radiation (e.g. visible light, thermal infra red etc.) from the Earth's surface, or actively transmit radiation and measure the reflected signal (e.g. at radar and radio frequencies).

Ground based techniques are used to monitor variations in soil gas emanation, SO_2 flux, gravity and magnetic fields, ground resistivity and conductivity, seismicity and deformation. Affordable, reliable techniques are being developed to make volcano monitoring a viable option in poorer countries (Rymer, 1993).

Although seismology will remain the most important monitoring tool for the foreseeable future, integration of seismic data with results from other methods such as geodesy, gravity, electrical, gas and temperature flux etc. is a much more powerful way of identifying eruption precursors. Smart systems using artificial neural networks (ANNs) are now being developed to integrate the vast quantities of data resulting from technological developments, to produce the simplest, best fitting models consistent with as much of the data as possible (Cristaldi et al., 1997). The priority now in volcano monitoring is the acquisition of more data and the development of rapid and reliable methods to collate, analyse and interpret them (McNutt et al., 2000). As well as technological and scientific advances, effective communication and interaction between volcanologists, civil authorities and the affected population are required to improve volcanic disaster mitigation.

5. Hazard mitigation

The 1991-1993 eruption of Etna was never a significant hazard to human lives, but the economic threat to the town of Zafferana Etnea was very real as the lava flow threatened to cut off roads and destroy property. The decision to intervene in a volcanic crisis such as this is not easy. If by diverting the lava flow away from one property another is threatened, the situation may actually be made worse. It is therefore a balance of probabilities and economics that determines the course of action as well as local politics and scientific judgement.

Lavas are not the only hazards that can be mitigated against. Eruption drills are rehearsed regularly at Japanese schools affected by volcanic ash; the emergency kit that children are taught to carry includes a helmet to protect them from falling ash. Also in Japan, sabo works are located on the flanks of many active volcanoes where lahars are expected when ash combines with rainfall to produce a deadly torrent of fluidised mud. Sabo works channel and to some extent control the rate of the flow but do not stop it. Automated systems at the summit of many hazardous volcanoes around the world send signals when some threshold limit is exceeded, affording people living below vital time for evacuation.

Although the effects of some eruptions can be reduced to some extent, evacuation is the only solution in most cases. On average, about 50,000 people are temporarily evacuated per year in an attempt to reduce the loss of life in an eruption. This figure has remained remarkably constant since 1976, although the eruption of Pinatubo in 1991 and the evacuation of some 250,000 people produces a significant 'blip' in the data (Figure 1). The number of deaths per year over the same period remains at a few tens except for the tragedy at Nevado del Ruiz in 1985 when 22,000 were killed by a mud flow. One reason for the loss of life at Herculaneum in AD79, was that once people realised the need to leave, roads out of town were blocked by ash. The sea was the most obvious means of escape once inland roads became impassable, but there would not have been enough ships available for everyone and the wind was blowing onshore at the time so that sailing boats were effectively trapped. Thus even when evacuation is the agreed course of action, it is a far from trivial solution. Evacuation plans already exist for many cities expected to be affected by volcanic activity in the future. In the case of Naples, which could be affected by Vesuvius or a reactivation of the Campi Flegrei caldera, the plan has come under considerable criticism because of the way in which it divides the city and its inhabitants and allocates them to various regions of Italy for sanctuary. The critics claim that the plan is socially destructive (Dobran, 1999). At least there is a plan for this major city though; many large towns and cities that may be affected in the next decade have no contingency plans at all.

6. Conclusions

Historically, volcanic activity has been considered to be primarily of local interest because typically, with the exception of large, infrequent explosive events, eruptions seriously affect only a few square km at most. However as world population continues to grow, more and more people live and work in expanding megacities and thus more and more people are at risk from the direct or indirect impact of volcanic eruptions. In addition to the immediate hazards posed by eruptive products to life, property and food production, volcanic activity of any kind may have a significant effect on the economy. During minor eruptions, tourism may increase and boost the local economy. The loss of farm lands, accommodation, communication and service infrastructure (roads, ports, water supplies, electric cables etc.) and permanent changes in the local ground water and drainage system can have severe economic consequences. A volcanic disaster on one side of the world can now have a significant economic impact on countries on the other. Insurance companies are particularly vulnerable because of this, but governments are also at risk. The National Plan for volcanic emergencies at Mount Vesuvius for example forecasts that around 700,000 people would need to be evacuated during a period of unrest preceding an explosive eruption such as the one that occurred in 1631 AD. The cost of evacuation and resettlement would represent a significant fraction of Italy's GNP and the rest of the EU would certainly suffer economically from such an event.

There are many larger populations living near active or potentially active volcanoes around the world. For example, Mount Rainer threatens Seattle and Silicon Valley, while Popocatepetl threatens Mexico City. Every year about 60 volcanoes erupt, most of them pass without notice in countries such as the UK, which have no active volcanoes. On average, there is an eruption once each decade comparable in size to the 1980 eruption of Mount St Helens, which was a local catastrophe with devastation over hundreds of km2. Once each century, there is an eruption similar to the 1883 eruption of Krakatoa, which was a regional catastrophe. Only once or twice each millennium is there a globally significant event comparable with the 1815 eruption of Tambora which caused global cooling and crop failure on the other side of the world. Much larger eruptions would likely produce global catastrophes and even mass extinctions, but the time between them is in excess of hundreds of thousands of years.

As we near the end of the International Decade for Natural Disaster Reduction (IDNDR), one of the lessons that has been well learnt is that disaster preparedness is crucial. The degree of effective communication between scientists and local officials and the public is the key to success or failure in the mitigation of a natural disaster such as a major volcanic eruption.

References

Cristaldi, M. Langer, H. and Nunnari, G. 1997. Inverse and on-line modelling. In Ferrucci, F. (ed.) TEKVOLC — Technique and Method Innovation in Geophysical Research, Monitoring and Early Warning at Active Volcanoes. Commission of European Communities Environment Program Interim report. Contract ENV4 CT95.

Dobran, F. 1999. http://idt.net/~dobran/HPrest.html#section2

McNutt., S., Rymer, H. and Stix, J. 2000. Synthesis of volcano monitoring. In Encyclopedia of Volcanoes (Sigurdsson, H., Houghton, B., McNutt, S., Rymer, H., Stix, J. eds.) Academic Press, San Diego, California, USA.

Rymer, H., 1993. Predicting volcanic eruptions using micro-gravity, and the mitigation of volcanic hazard. In Natural Disasters. (Merriman, P.A. and Browitt, C.W.A. eds.) Thomas Telford, London, UK. pp 252-269.

Simkin, T. and Siebert, L. 1994. Volcanoes of the World. Geoscience Press, Inc. Tucson, Arizona, USA. pp 349.

Tanguy, J.-C., Ribiere, Ch., Scarth, A. and Tjetjep, W.S. 1998. Victims from volcanic eruptions: a revised database. Bull. Volcanol. 60; 137-144.

Tilling, R. 1989. Introduction and overview. In Volcanic Hazards. Short course in volcanology. Volume 1. (ed. R.Tilling) American Geophysical Union. 1-8.

GROUNDWATER RESOURCES - CONTINUING PRESSURE ON A MAJOR NATURAL RESOURCE

John Mather,
Department of Geology,
Royal Holloway, University of London, Egham, Surrey, TW20 0EX

1. Introduction

If the water locked up in polar ice is excluded, groundwater represents some 97% of the Earth's freshwater resources. Worldwide it supplies at least 1.5 million urban dwellers with their water supply and is extensively utilised by rural communities for both domestic supplies and irrigation. In Europe around 60% of potable supplies are derived from groundwater. In England and Wales, as a whole, the percentage is rather less at just over 33% but in the south-east this rises to over 70%.

Traditionally this water was both reliable and pure, particularly in comparison to surface sources. Because of the large storage capacity of many aquifers, water supplies were able to survive periods of drought, continuing to supply water which could be distributed to customers with little treatment. The combination of a natural storage reservoir and the lack of significant treatment costs also meant that groundwater was a cheap source of water for public supply.

However, over the last 25 years this situation has changed dramatically. Both quantity and quality are coming under increasing pressure as demand for water increases and intensive agricultural production and industrial use of chemicals impact on the water environment. Unfortunately groundwater generally moves very slowly and is only seen where boreholes have been drilled or when springs discharge at the surface. This lack of visibility means that problems can take many years to appear by which time damage may be widespread and, with respect to water quality, sometimes irreversible. This paper will identify the main issues and problems which can he classified into two broad categories: those affecting groundwater yields and those affecting groundwater quality.

2. Groundwater Yields

Recharge to groundwater occurs through rainfall or melting snow which moves down through the soil until it reaches the water table below which the rocks are saturated with water. In Britain recharge occurs during the winter months from October to April. Between May and September, no matter how much it rains, only in exceptional circumstances does recharge occur. This is because all the rainfall is used up by growing plants or returns to the atmosphere by evaporation in the warmer summer weather. It is therefore the winter rainfall which is important and if this does not fall in sufficient quantities groundwater levels are inevitably lower than anticipated the following summer. Now as well as providing water for public supply groundwater also maintains river flows and supports wetlands and marshes. If groundwater did not continuously feed surface watercourses many would disappear in dry weather. Thus the water companies together with the Environment Agency have the difficult task of maintaining water supplies whilst also conserving river flows and wetland habitats. The southeast of England is the area of the country with the highest reliance on groundwater and over the last 25 years a number of severe droughts have made this task much more difficult. Low winter rainfall in 1975-76, 1988-92 and 1995-97 resulted in low groundwater levels and in some areas immediately north of London groundwater levels in observation boreholes were the lowest ever recorded (Figure 1).

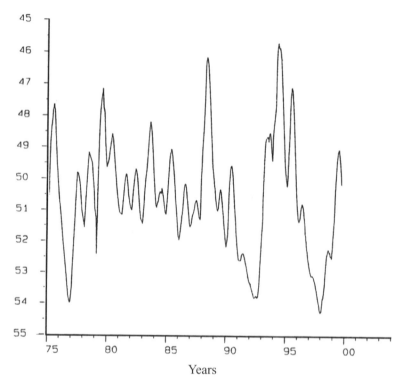

Figure 1. Hydrograph from an observation well at The Holt, between Whitwell and Kimpton in Hertfordshire (Grid ref: TL 1696 1964) during the years 1975-1999. Vertical scale represents the groundwater level in metres below an arbitrary datum. (Data supplied by the Environment Agency).

The need of water companies to maintain water supplies means that the low groundwater levels have had a major impact on river flows in south-east England. The headwaters of Chalk streams have always seen intermittent flows, that is to say, their point of origin has varied greatly at one time being a long way down the valley, at another time at a much higher elevation. The source of the River Ver in Hertfordshire, for example, varied by at least 5 miles in the last century well before extensive abstraction from the Chalk aquifer began. However, the low water levels in 1988-92 meant that many Chalk streams had little flow in them for two or more years causing considerable loss of river amenity.

The recent apparent increase in drought frequency suggests either that the climate is changing in response to global warming or that it is the result of natural variability in rainfall patterns which the relatively short period of historic records does not accurately represent. The current variations in the rainfall pattern are broadly in line with some predictions of the impact of climate change. If it is accepted that climate change is the cause, groundwater levels are likely to remain subject to wide fluctuations and the implications for water supplies and wetland habitats are significant.

If both groundwater supplies and river flows are to be preserved what options are available? Clearly leakage reduction, metering and demand management will have a part to play, but more use can also be made of the storage provided by the aquifers themselves. If water levels are lowered, storage space is created which could be exploited by artificial recharge. If this is not viable, potable water might be injected into urban aquifers, where quality is poor, at times of surplus and recovered at times of need. In many urban areas groundwater levels are currently rising and at the Trafalgar Square observation borehole in London, for example, this rise is 2.5m per year (Figure 2). Such urban groundwaters are generally less pure than traditional groundwaters.

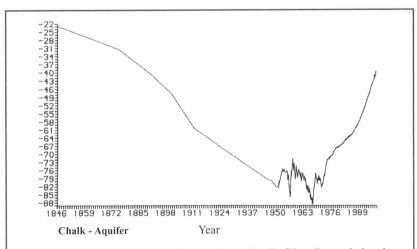

Figure 2 - Hydrograph from an observation well at Trafalgar Square in London (Grid ref: TQ 2996 8051) during the years 1846-1997. Vertical scale represents the groundwater level in metres above Ordnance Datum (Data from the Environment Agency).

However, they could be used to supplement river flows thus preserving higher quality groundwater for potable water supplies. For example London groundwaters could be used to supplement the flow of the Thames and its tributaries and groundwater beneath Birmingham used to supplement the flow of the Trent.

3. Groundwater Quality

The International Association of Hydrogeologists have identified the main sources of potential pollution as urban development, industrial processes and agricultural practices. Problems are both historical arising from industries which began production in the 19th century, and current, arising from modern methods of intensive agriculture. Pollution arises both from point sources and from diffuse sources where it is not possible to identify and quantify individual contributions resulting in the deterioration in groundwater quality.

Groundwater pollution from point sources in England and Wales was collated by the Environment Agency in 1995. Landfill sites are numerically the most significant point source but in terms of their actual impacts on groundwater are considered to be somewhat less of a problem than sources such as old gasworks, dry cleaning facilities and engineering works. A total of 1205 point sources of pollution were identified. 24% of these were impacting on the Chalk with a further 19% on the Permo-Triassic Sandstones. Thus there were some 518 probable contamination incidents from point sources involving the two most important aquifers in England and Wales.

Among the most significant of the point source pollutants are the light non-aqueous phase liquids (LNAPLs) and their dense cousins (DNAPLs). In both cases the free product will dissolve into the groundwater over a period of years. The LNAPLs, generally petroleum hydrocarbons, originate from spillages or leaking tanks and float as a pancake at the water table (Figure 3). Many petrol filling stations, once investigated, have proved to give rise to pollution and in the USA tests on petroleum tanks and pipelines found a 30% leakage rate. Problems are much more severe in former Eastern Bloc countries as a result of the indiscriminate exploitation of resources and the extraction of every ounce of industrial production from worn out and inefficient plant. For example around the city of Ploesti in Romania up to 8 metres of oil float on the surface of the water table as a result of leakage from pipelines and storage tanks belonging to a network of refineries. The DNAPLs, generally organic solvents, tend to migrate rapidly downwards towards the base of an aquifer (Figure 3). In addition to contaminating large volumes of groundwater DNAPLs degrade to form other hazardous substances such as vinyl chloride that are a threat to human health. Solvents are used as degreasing agents at industrial sites such as tanneries, factories involved in the manufacture and assembly of automotive components, printing works and airfields and many pollution incidents have come to light over the past 20 years involving both the Chalk and Permo-Triassic Sandstone aquifers.

It can be argued that these point sources of contamination are possible to control and remediate. For example legislation and regulations can be introduced to control the storage and use of both LNAPLs and DNAPLs and spills can be cleaned up using containment followed by pump and treat or bioremediation.

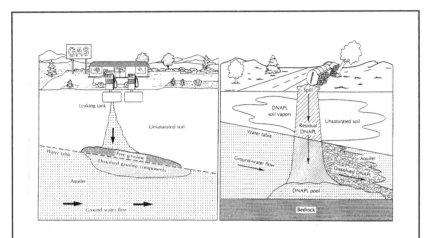

Figure 3 - Spillage of, at left, gasoline which is lighter than water and which is denser than water and sinks to the base of the aquifer. Both concentrate near the water table and at right chlorinated solvent are only sparingly soluble in water. (Diagrams) from fetter, C.W. 1994. *Applied Hydrogeology,* 3rd Edition. Macmillan. New York).

The most difficult field is that of diffuse pollution, particularly from modern farming practices. Nitrate, from the intensive use of fertilizers, pesticides and herbicides are all found in groundwaters and in some parts of Britain nitrate concentrations exceed regulatory limits. Solutions involve radical changes in land use which may have a real impact on conventional farming practices. On a local scale specific sources can be targeted and some Nitrate Sensitive Zones have been created. However, to effect a long term solution innovative policy changes are required which value the preservation of water resources as highly as food production.

4. The Future

There is no doubt that the future will see increasing pressure on groundwater resources in England and Wales. The situation in North Hertfordshire can be taken as a typical example of the problems ahead. Ten thousand new homes are earmarked for greenbelt land between Stevenage and Hitchin early next century. This land is situated on the Chalk aquifer from which the local water supply is principally derived. Two of the main streams in Hitchin, the Oughten and Hiz already suffer from flows and need to be augmented from pumped sources. The new development will mean that yet more water is needed increasing the demand on the Chalk aquifer. Urbanisation of the Chalk will change recharge patterns and increase the potential for contamination. The overall effect on the Chalk aquifer and the local water environment can only be negative, yet such considerations do not seem to be a significant consideration within the planning process.

The future appears bleak, innovative developments and radical changes will be needed if the attractive groundwater-fed streams of southern England are to continue to flow and groundwater is to remain a pure source of potable water.

CAN THE EARTH SAFELY CONTAIN OUR DANGEROUS WASTES?

Sir John Knill FGS F.R.Eng

Highwood Farm, Long Lane, Shaw-cum-Donnington, Newbury, Berkshire RG14 2TB

All biological activity results in the production of waste. Since the very first existence of life in the form of the earliest primitive bacteria thousands of millions of years ago, the Earth has been influenced by the waste produced by the plants and animals which live on and below its surface. The geological record is punctuated by rocks which are the products of waste accumulation. Because such wastes were of natural origin, they were effectively innocuous decaying to be re-used as a habitat or nutrient. Indeed much of the chemistries of the oceans and atmosphere which have been, and are, critical to evolution and to the existence of Man, are the product of such waste-forming processes.

Life has co-existed with waste for a long time and we would not survive unless we, in our turn, also generated waste. But can we live as comfortably with our waste as did our ancestors? There is a tendency for over-reaction and emotion about waste in the modern world although to most it is best regarded as out of sight and out of mind. The essential truth is that waste is here to stay, and it needs to be managed properly and safely.

Man is now a major producer of the waste products which are having a significant influence on the global system. Although many of the earliest cities of the near East were built on layers of rubbish known as tells, civilisations were overwhelmed by a misuse of resources rather than by their unwanted products. This situation continued for millennia. Nevertheless the sanitary conditions in towns and cities, and particularly water quality, left much to be desired. It was not until the nineteenth century with the coming of the industrial revolution that waste began to be more widely dispersed away from the sites of its generation in the form of discernible pollution of the air and watercourses. In 1896 Aarhenius perceptively pointed out that the burning of fossil fuels might increase atmospheric carbon dioxide, and so change the global radiation balance. However, it was not until the 1930s that it was convincingly shown that atmospheric carbon dioxide was on the increase, and that such man made pollution encompassed the Earth. Thirty years later, less than half a century ago, Rachel Carson's book The Silent Spring alerted the world to the catastrophic influences on wildlife of the widespread application of DDT and pesticides.

A burgeoning world population and technological advance will inevitably ensure that the quantity, diversity and potential sources of waste will increase. Vast concentrations of waste will accumulate around and in the megacities of the Third World which will be inhabited by some 60% of the expected increase in the world population. Technological advance has now created stable, exotic wastes and these will not readily break down in the natural environment into safe products.

What, then, are all these wastes? The total annual solid waste arisings in the UK are in excess of 500 million tonnes. About a quarter of these wastes come from quarrying and mining, with dredged wastes forming about 10% of the total. About one third of these are Controlled Wastes which include household, industrial, commercial and demolition wastes, together with sewage sludge when incinerated or disposed of to landfill. Much of this waste material, such as paper, cardboard, metal and some builders' rubble, is effectively inert.

To place these figures in further context a single large coal-fired power station emits each year some 11 million tonnes of carbon dioxide and about 200,000 tonnes of sulphur dioxide and nitrous oxide. The weight of unseen gaseous wastes rival the solid wastes. In addition almost a million tonnes of coal ash is produced, concentrating trace substances such as mercury, arsenic, carbon and uranium all of which have the potential to be released into the atmosphere.

The more dangerous wastes, whose disposal needs greater precautions, include those whose toxic, corrosive or flammable properties are long-lived and will not degenerate with time. Such wastes come in a variety of forms including acids, solvents, PCBs, cyanides, dioxins, a wide range of liquids and sludges, metallic residues, contaminated soils, and medical and radioactive wastes.

How then have such wastes been disposed of? The atmosphere, rivers, lakes and the sea have formed favourite disposal sites providing the advantages of both removing, and diluting, the waste. With both the spread and increase in sites of population, as well as inter-continental transport by air and water, the opportunity for wider dissemination of waste around the globe by such means has increased. The concept of "dilute and disperse" which was for many decades regarded as a proper method of waste disposal is now largely discredited.

The atmosphere transmits gaseous and energy fluxes around the Earth rapidly, having a remarkably short memory of a few tens of days. A plume of fine ash rising from an erupting volcano takes very little time to circumnavigate the globe. It is therefore not surprising that global protocols have now been developed for the control of gaseous pollutants which can have widespread environmental impacts. The recognition that CFCs had effectively depleted stratospheric ozone above the Antarctic was rapidly followed by international restraints on their use and disposal. But it is only in the last fifteen years that such cross-boundary resolve has begun to tackle such serious issues.

In contrast the ocean climate has a longer potential life of some tens of years, with little ocean water remaining in coherent masses for greater than about fifty years. As a result the ocean, another traditional repository for liquid and solid waste, is also an effective, albeit slower, transmitter and diluter. In the shelf sea areas, such as the North Sea, where there is restricted circulation, pollution can accumulate both in water and sea-bed sediments. However, in the open ocean dilution can be effective because of the enormous fluid volumes. Solid materials dropped onto or into the deep sea floor are relatively remote from the near-surface oceanic and terrestrial food chain. Robust scientific safety cases have demonstrated that the open, deep oceans have some capacity for waste disposal. However, international agreements have now recognised that such ocean disposal of waste is publicly unacceptable.

As a result of simple elimination the land masses are now regarded as the proper site for the disposal of most wastes. Technologies need be developed to ensure pollution-free and safe containment. The philosophy of responsible waste disposal has moved on from that of "dilute and disperse" to one of "concentrate and contain" with the ability to "disarm and destroy" some of the more intractable wastes. Waste minimisation, segregation, streaming, conditioning and packaging all contribute to more effective ways of managing different waste forms. Similarly protection zones can be identified on geological and hydrogeological criteria which can ensure that the effects of waste disposal or the dispersion of potential pollutants (e.g. pesticides, agricultural fertilisers) on the environment can be minimised. However, ultimately, responsible waste disposed of within the environment relies either on geological containment, or entrapment within a geological sink such as shallow water sediments, to avoid re-circulation. The demonstration of geological containment is central to effective long-term environmental waste management.

The traditional method of solid waste disposal on land has been landfill. Sites have been selected on many grounds, the least frequent being that of an over-riding technical suitability. Typically the sites have to be large and relatively convenient to the source of waste. Abandoned quarries, pits and low-value land have been particularly favoured. Many waste types, notably domestic waste, are unstable continuing to decompose in situ, releasing methane gas from wood products as well as noxious leachates. Older landfill sites were not engineered so that leachate percolated freely from the landfill into its foundations, joining the groundwater system and developing a pollution plume. Commonly more toxic wastes were disposed of within the core of the fill; liquid wastes were disposed of in lagoons overlying absorbent paper-rich waste. Later landfill sites tended to avoid aquifers, being located on clays or similar less permeable formations which retained the leachate, or discharged it into local watercourses.

Modern landfill sites are built upon multi-layer membranes within which a layer of high-density polyethylene (HDPE) provides a thin barrier of low permeability. Leachate formed in the decomposing waste is drained through the landfill, collected and then treated prior to disposal. The extensive use of polythene bags for containment of waste results, if the bags are buried, in the creation of individual bio-reactors which may delay the rate of landfill decay. It is also practice to cut such bags open, comminuting the contents on the landfill surface prior to disposal. Soil layers and vertical pipe drains provide for internal drainage of fluid and gas generated by the decay process. The objective of such an approach to landfill disposal is to encourage the rate of decay attempting to create an effectively sterile waste mass before the HDPE membrane eventually fails after a few decades. Because of concerns regarding the permanence of membrane stability, some engineered barriers incorporate clay linings which provide for improved containment as well as enhanced attenuation of pollutants. Remediation of existing landfills has built on such principles by the introduction of clay-filled trenches which provide containment and retain lateral flow of pollutant. On-going remediation may become a standard feature of unintentionally long-lived landfills.

The most stringent requirements for landfill occur where the waste to be disposed of consists of toxic materials. One approach has been to chemically stabilise liquid wastes so that they are retained in situ in a solid form and cannot be transported by groundwater. Elsewhere disposal of liquid wastes has been carried out down mine shafts and into boreholes to remove the waste from near-surface environmental processes.

The deep disposal of waste in engineered cavities below the Earth's surface has become, for the nuclear industry, the preferred method of disposing of intermediate and high level radioactive wastes; such techniques are likely to be used for a wider range of waste types. Extensive investigations for such repositories have been carried out, in several countries and in differing geological conditions, into the feasibility of such disposal methods. International protocols constrain the cross-boundary movement of such dangerous wastes but this inevitably prevents the best geological conditions being made available for international repositories. The considerable length of time over which such wastes will remain toxic raises serious questions. Slow geological processes would still have the potential to recycle waste components back into the near-surface environment within thousands or tens of thousands of years.

None of the modern methods of waste disposal will remove the waste from our environment for ever. In each case there is an element of pragmatism which balances the rate at which the waste will become sterile, as against the speed of geological processes which might return the waste to the ground surface. Because we live in a world that is driven by short-term thinking, long-term environmental issues, such as selecting locations for waste disposal, tend to get short shrift from politicians and the public alike. If this generation is to meet its responsibilities to future generations then such attitudes will need to adapt. To ensure such greater public understanding and acceptability geologists must refine their ability to predict the consequences of environmental processes and impacts, not only in the past, but also in the present and future. By such means we can offer a major contribution to sustaining a global quality of life.

GEOLOGY AND WASTE - FLUIDS IN THE ENVIRONMENT

Jeremy Joseph FGS

11 Mallory Avenue, Caversham, Reading, Berkshire, RG4 7QN

1. Introduction

All processes produce waste, regardless of whether they are entirely natural or man has a hand in them. The difference is that natural processes are generally more efficient, in other words they to produce less waste, than those devised by man. Waste is material - or energy - which has no further use and needs to be returned to the environment. This is true whether the process is natural or man made.

There is nothing wrong in the production of waste. All materials and energy came from the environment in the first place and all must eventually return there. What is wrong is allowing waste to cause harm. If harm is to be avoided, waste must be returned to the environment in a form and at a rate which the environment can accept. That is the way in which the environment has survived through geological time and that is how we should aim to treat it, too.

2. Generating Waste

Ever since the first tools were made man has been generating process wastes outside nature. Some of the earliest remains are probably rough piles of stone chips from knapping hand tools. Before that came piles of bones from food.

Piles and scatters of waste are not nice to live with. They get in the way and, if they include food waste, they soon begin to smell and attract flies. It makes sense to tidy waste away.

There are piles and holes filled with waste associated with human sites dating far back into pre-history. Many are small and might have served single families or village-like communities. As communities grew it became inconvenient to collect waste in small heaps and pits locally. It could be done, it still is, but some groups found that they disliked the effect that this had on their lives. The rubbish tip was born. It was somewhere to put waste that was a little bit away from where people lived or worked, usually at the edge of the village or just outside the town. Until recently it was acceptable to put almost anything but sewage or bodies onto a rubbish tip.

Rubbish tips are found wherever there has been civilisation. They are associated with the ancient cities of Sumeria, Persia and the Roman Empire, the Aztecs, mediaeval Europe and all other cultures. One of the oldest tips known in Britain is on Salisbury Plain. It was found and excavated in the 1990s but is around 3000 years old and dates from the Bronze Age. It seems to be associated with a regular festival of some sort and is made up largely of food waste - meat (lamb) bones, shell fish remains, etc. Obviously the locals found the smell and the flies offensive because they seem to have covered the waste from each year with a layer of soil. As towns and cities grew over the centuries so did the rubbish dumps. The real limitation was transport. It was available but waste tends to be bulky and is not very easy to move. Because of this the dumps and tips tended to be near population centres. As cities got bigger society was also becoming richer, which led to even greater increases in the amounts thrown away. Waste was reused and recycled extensively - even in the Middle Ages - but still the tips grew. At the same time, increasing and more complex levels of industry produced greater amounts of more complex and unpleasant wastes. The problem was no longer one of relatively small amounts of seemingly harmless materials.

For the future we need more efficient processes which produce less waste. Where waste cannot be avoided, we may need to think about the form it takes. In some cases it may be possible to change a process so that the waste is easier to use elsewhere. We also need to understand more about the behaviour of different wastes and how we can manage them to maximise benefit and minimise harm. The rest of this paper is about some of the things that we have learnt.

3. Types of waste and what happens to them

Solid wastes, the things you put into a dustbin, can be divided into two main types, depending on whether they are inert or not. Inert wastes do not react in normal circumstances. They may not be very beautiful but they do not smell or ooze and they tend to stay where they are put.

Wastes that are not inert can be degraded, in other words they can and do react. Because of this they can cause harm in the environment and so they need to be managed. Problems can occur as the fluids - the liquids and gases - move through the waste and away from it into the environment. It is the gases and liquids that come from or pass through the wastes that make the pollutants mobile. They carry a great variety of chemicals with them.

Gases are generated particularly during the biological degradation of waste. They can carry large amounts of material away. They need to be contained and channelled so that they can be treated. Many gases are produced but only two - methane and carbon dioxide - are of general importance. Little can be done about carbon dioxide at present, although storage may be possible in the future - if that is worthwhile. Methane can be treated by burning - perhaps in an engine or fuel cell to generate power - which converts it to carbon dioxide. Methane is more important as a greenhouse gas than carbon dioxide, so there is benefit from the conversion and very often from recovering the energy as power, too.

The liquids - the non-gaseous, usually water-based, fluids - that come from degrading wastes often have the potential to cause harm (see Figure 1). Like the gases, they need to be managed and controlled if they are to be treated and their potential for harm reduced to a low level.

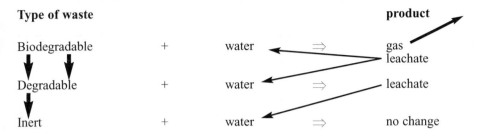

Figure 1 - the ways that waste can degrade

The liquid (the water) in a swimming pool is managed by containment. The same can be done with a landfill by making the sides and base as nearly water-tight as possible. Modern landfills are rather like fruit or meat pies. They have a skin for containment (see Figure 2) and hold a mixture of liquids and solids that react and (if you do not eat the pie) degrades slowly.

Geological materials can be used to help with the problems. They can be used to contain or hold the waste, sometimes they can also be used to react with pollutants to make them less harmful.

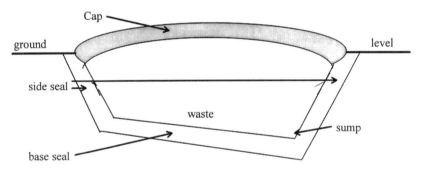

Figure 2 - simplified section through a land fill.

The gases can be prevented from escaping through the top or side of the site by using caps and side seals. These may be made of clay or plastic - itself manufactured from oil. The gases are channelled to collection points through the waste or, better still, along drains formed from layers of gravel or other inert lumps. When methane does escape and mixes with oxygen it can explode, as happened in 1986 at Loscoe in Derbyshire – it is important to keep it under control.

The first stage of managing liquids, like gases, is to contain them. (The liquid that flows through or forms in waste in a landfill is called leachate.) Management is only possible if the landfill is contained. The length of time for which the containment is needed depends on local circumstances. It is important to remember, however, that no fluid - liquid or gas - can be contained for ever. All systems and structures, however good and strong they seem when new will break down eventually. When containment systems break down or fail they leak. (Equally, of course, it is not possible to keep any liquid out perpetually. The idea of keeping waste dry and in store for ever is nonsense; it cannot work.) The aim must be to treat the leachate while the containment system is working, ie before it starts to leak badly.

Containment systems can be designed fairly easily for fluid management. They must be strong so that they last a reasonable length of time and they must be good enough to hold the liquid and gases involved.

4. Containment

Ideally, the material used for containment must form a strong, flexible, barrier which is water and gas proof. If it is to work effectively, it must have three properties.

1. It must resist attack by the leachate inside the waste body and any groundwaters outside If it cannot do so, leachate may be released into the local environment when it fails.

2. It must provide a reasonable level of containment. None of the materials that can be used to contain large volumes for long periods are completely water or gas-proof. On the whole, though, they leak so slowly that the amount of material entering the environment in leachate causes no harm. The containment that they provide lasts long enough to allow time for the fluids from the waste to be collected and treated.

3. The material must be both strong and flexible enough to resist damage caused by changing loadings and support. Over long periods, for instance, parts of the ground beneath the base of the site may settle at different rates.

The most obvious natural - geological - material to use for containment is clay. The particles are very small and it is relatively easy to engineer to provide leachate containment. If the engineered clay is reasonably thick - one metre is typical - it forms a resilient and slightly flexible barrier. Fluids move very slowly through such barriers into the environment.

The clay must be engineered carefully if the system is to work successfully. Clay is placed in layers, called lifts. These are made thin enough, often 200 to 250 mm, to ensure that the energy from the rollers goes right through and forces them together. The containment is of little use if it includes planes of weakness, along which liquids can move easily, at the junctions between lifts. Equally, if the clay is too wet or too dry, it may be difficult to work to obtain the best engineering and containment properties. It is important, for instance, that all the lumps of clay (the clods) are squeezed together so that, like the lifts, there are no gaps between them for fluids to move through. It will not matter how good a seal the clay within the clods can provide if fluids are able to flow round them and get out into the environment (see Figure 3).

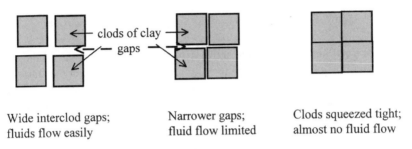

Wide interclod gaps; fluids flow easily

Narrower gaps; fluid flow limited

Clods squeezed tight; almost no fluid flow

Figure 3 - fluid movement between clods of clay.

5. Types of Clay

It is quite normal to talk about 'clay' as though there is only one sort. In fact, of course, there are very many and they all behave in slightly different ways. In waste management, however, the important differences are between the two main clay groups - the smectites and illites.

The smectites are the swelling clays. The best known examples are the montmorillonites or bentonites. When water is added to these clays the thin, platy, structure - the crystal lattice - expands and the body of clay grows out to squeeze into gaps and fill holes. This could be very useful in controlling and managing leachate if the clays always behaved in this way. The water used to make them expand is a very weak solution of salts and other chemicals. Leachate, however, is a strong or very strong solution and has a different effect. It attacks the smectite lattice and changes it into an illite form (see figure 4). The new-formed illite pulls together into little clumps (a process called agglomeration), which makes the clods much more leaky.

The changes to the smectite clays do not look or seem very large. The effects can be. Leachate will move very slowly through an engineered clay barrier at the bottom of a site. Typically, it might move one metre over a period of between thirty and three hundred years. If the smectite- - leachate reaction has occurred and there was much smectite in the original clay, the leakage rate might be reduced to between three months and three years for a metre of travel. This is still very slow but not slow enough to allow for all of the problems of management and treatment.

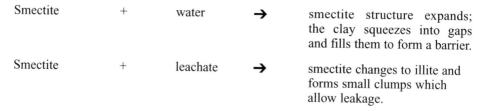

Figure 4 - what happens to smectite clays with leachate and water.

Illites do not swell and are fairly unreactive. If they form the main part of the clay used for containment they can be squeezed together into tight layers from the start. They are not affected by reactions with leachate - because they behave as though they have already reacted - so the leakiness of the layer does not generally increase when they are exposed to it.

6. Plastic Barriers

In some circumstances it may be necessary to use plastic to contain the waste, instead of clay or other natural materials. Usually this is because local minerals are not suitable for making the barrier. Very occasionally it is because of something in the waste. The decision to use plastic should depend on whether the environmental damage from making and using it is less than that caused by hauling clay to the site.

Two types of plastic have been used for landfill engineering over the years - PVC and HDPE. HDPE is by far the most common now. It comes as long, wide, sheets up to 2 mm thick that are welded together to form a leak-proof layer across the base and the sides of the site. Plastic can provide a good seal for the first few years - ten to fifty - if it is laid properly and has very few holes in it. It cannot be used on its own, however, and needs a fine mineral base.

Plastics have been seen as better than clays. They have their place and they do make it possible to control the fluids from waste where that might not be the case. On the other hand, they degrade with time - a typical life might be one hundred years - and so it is even more important to ensure that the fluids are managed and treated at reasonable speed and as quickly as possible.

7. Fluids in the Environment

So far, this paper has been about containing the fluids from wastes - the gases and liquids they generate - so that they can be treated. While the waste is degrading the fluids are capable of causing harm in the environment. The purpose of containment is to prevent this; the purpose of treatment is to change the fluids and the pollutants that they contain into forms which will cause the least harm and allow them to be released at a rate which the environment can accept.

Like all fluids, the fluids from degrading wastes follow gradients. Gases tend to move to areas of relatively low pressure. The gas, generated in the waste, is contained by the cap. Pressure builds up gradually in the landfill. If the side seal leaks, the gas will move into the surrounding rocks and follow fractures and fissures until it can escape completely. It is important that the gas is controlled - seeping gas at Loscoe exploded inside a house - to prevent it causing harm.

Leachate follows the gravity gradient and flows to the lowest point it can reach. In a landfill this is often somewhere on the base. The floor of the landfill is shown as a slope in figure 2 because landfills are usually designed to help the leachate to flow to a collection point or sump. This makes it possible to collect the liquid and treat it. If the liner leaks, leachate can escape into the environment. Like the gases, it travels along fractures and fissures because they form the easiest path to follow.

Unlike gas, leachate generally moves downward until it joins the groundwater. While the waste degrades, which can take a very long time (tens of years), leachate fresh from the landfill contains many substances which can cause harm. If the rate of leakage is low enough, the leachate itself may degrade so that it is less harmful when it gets to the groundwater than it was when it left the landfill. Sometimes this degradation is caused by reactions outside the landfill, at others some of the pollutants may bind (adsorb) permanently onto mineral particles.

The number of contaminants and pollutants that can occur in leachates is great and their effects are very variable. Amongst other things it must be remembered that a compound which acts as a contaminant in one place may cause no harm elsewhere. As an example, a clean but strong solution of sodium chloride would be no problem in the sea but, equally, would cause real harm if released into streams and rivers, or groundwaters. In other words, local circumstances have to be taken into account. There is no point at all in allowing harm that might be avoided, in fact it would be irresponsible to do so. As with the gas, the purpose of the side and base seals of a landfill is to prevent leachate from reaching fractures and fissures in the surrounding strata.

8. Monitoring and Pollution

The environment around all landfills is monitored nowadays to check whether any of the fluids have escaped. It is always hoped, of course, that nothing will be found. If that is the case then all of the containment - the base and side seals, and the cap - is probably working.

The sampling process has to be designed to take account of changes in time and space. One of the most important things is to start taking samples before waste is placed. This allows some estimate of the natural state of the environment in the area before it is disturbed by the landfill. The environment is not static, although it may seem to be, and these early samples have to be spread over a reasonable time scale if they are to provide useful information. The standard recommendation is a minimum of at least a year, so that the full cycle of seasons is covered; in many cases more would be better. Once started, sampling needs to be done frequently and regularly until the fluids passing through the waste - landfill gas and leachate - have no more potential to cause harm. At that point the waste is in equilibrium with the local environment.

The environment itself is constantly changing, so the same applies to sampling around the area. Contamination can only move when fluids flow along gradients (see above). It is important to monitor down the gradient from the landfill, to see if changes are occurring that might have been caused by the landfill. It is equally important to monitor in other directions to see if other things in the local environment are causing change. As an example, it would be foolish - and could harm the environment - if major work was done at a landfill to deal with contamination whose source was then found to be elsewhere.

Streams and rivers (surface waters) are monitored by taking samples directly from them. Gas, on the other hand, is monitored on the ground surface and, like groundwater, in boreholes. The most difficult thing is to work out where to take the samples. They need to be representative of the environment and what is happening to it. At the same time, some of them need to be taken from places where contamination is most likely to occur - or to cause the most problems - if there is a leak. The job of placing sampling points is difficult, interesting and important.

9. Concluding Remarks

This paper is about waste and geology. Contaminants are only mobile when they are carried along with fluids. Waste management and landfill design is really about containing the fluids, and doing so for sufficiently long to allow them to be collected and treated. If that can be done it should be possible to minimise the harm caused or even to avoid harm altogether.

Although the paper is only about contaminants from waste in landfill there are very many other possible sources. Almost everything that man does can lead to pollution. Almost always the answer is better management of the processes and very often geology contains the key.

Acknowledgements

The author is greatly indebted to Cally Oldershaw for her help and advice with this paper.

AIR POLLUTION
THE EVER-CHANGING THREAT

J.N.B. Bell

Professor of Environmental Pollution
Department of Biology/T.H. Huxley School of Environment, Earth Sciences & Engineering, Imperial College at Silwood Park, Ascot, Berkshire SL5 7PY

1. Introduction

Air pollution represents a particularly insidious threat to both human health and the environment in that many highly damaging forms of it are effectively invisible and their serious adverse consequences not readily detected in the absence of sophisticated and expensive research programmes. The history of air pollution has been one of ever increasing scales and changing nature, as reductions in one type in response to emission controls is counteracted by the appearance of new forms of pollutant. The earliest recorded cases of concern over air pollution occurred in ancient Rome, where the smoky air was believed to have damaging effects on human health. Subsequently the introduction of coal-burning into European cities from Medieval times onwards led to growing problems, which have only been controlled in recent years. Now the major concerns in the developed world are associated, directly or indirectly, with motor vehicle derived pollution. While major studies are being made in controlling pollution in the developed world, in most developing countries rapid industrialisation and growth of motor traffic are leading to massive increases in emissions, with accompanying health and environmental effects. Originally air pollution was a highly localised problem, but since the beginning of the Industrial Revolution it has progressively increased in scale, becoming regional, then international and finally completely global. In this paper the story of air pollution will be examined, in particular looking at how the lessons learned from the past can help us to avoid similar problems in the future. At a conference organised by the Geologists' Association, it is worth noting that the vast bulk of air pollution arises ultimately from the utilisation by man of materials derived from the Earth's crust.

2. Air Pollution 1200-1970

I shall use the UK primarily for this historical review. Here in the UK the story of air pollution really starts in 1285 when a law was passed to ban burning of coal in London, as a result of increasing amounts of this fuel being shipped from early collieries of north east England (hence "Sea Coal Lane" in the City of London). Initially the coal was used for industrial purposes, such as brewing and lime production, but after 400 years became employed increasingly in domestic fires. Our best information on the situation at this time comes from the publication in 1661 by the noted English diarist, John Evelyn, of his book "Fumzifugium: or the Inconvenience of the Aer and Smoake of London Dissipated". This author described in graphic detail the appalling effects of London's smoke pollution on human health, vegetation and materials. He also noted the results of the earliest experiment, albeit inadvertent, in removing air pollution to observe any consequent changes: the English Civil War resulted in the siege of Newcastle Upon Tyne, cutting off London's coal supplies. Evelyn described the amazing consequences of the improvement in air quality with the flowers of London coming into bloom and the trees bearing fruit. The lessons which should have been learned from Evelyn's observations were not taken on board and coal smoke pollution worsened, with little official action taken to remedy the problem, although a major pressure body - the National Smoke Abatement Society - was founded in 1899. This body still exists in the form of the prestigious National Society for Clean Air and Environmental Protection, reflecting the fact that the issue remains high on the environmental agenda. Effectively nothing was done until, as so often is the case with environmental legislation, a disaster occurred whose political repercussions resulted in appropriate action. This disaster took the form of a heavy smog (coal smoke trapped in a fog) over London in early December 1952, and resulted in the premature deaths of at least 4,000 people, largely from exacerbation of chronic respiratory and circulatory illnesses. The resulting outcry produced the political pressure on the government to bring about the Clean Air Act of 1956, which provided the mechanisms for local authorities to introduce "Smokeless Zones", where the burning of bituminous coal was banned. Consequently the air quality of British cities showed a progressive and marked improvement, with visibility in winter increasing and smoke and sulphur dioxide levels falling to the extent that they are currently a fraction of those occurring in the recent past. While much of this was achieved by the legislation enacted in 1956, socio-economic factors also played an enormous role, with coal being replaced by natural gas and other cleaner fuels, clearance of slums and removal of industry from inner city areas.

3. The Emergence of New Urban Air Pollution Problems

With the massive improvement in air quality resulting from the decline in coal use, a most unfortunate complacency arose in official circles in the UK, with the assumption that air pollution presented no problem in either cities or the countryside. Indeed official government publications took on a self-congratulatory tone and research into health effects declined almost to zero. This was doubly unfortunate, as the 1970s and 1980s saw the growing realisation in other quarters that new air pollution problems were emerging, partly associated with increases in motor vehicle emissions and also that environmental damage could occur over large areas of countryside as a result of acid rain and tropospheric ozone. As the 1980s progressed it became apparent that air quality was deteriorating in cities, with growing emissions of nitrogen oxides (NOx) and tiny particulates from the ever increasing motor vehicle population. In December 1991, the national press contained such headlines as "The Return of the Smogs". This referred to an incident in London where these pollutants became trapped in fog, with many people reporting unpleasant symptoms, such as shortness of breath, and evidence of about 200 deaths more than normal. Since then interest has grown enormously in urban air pollution, with large research programmes being developed into health effects and the atmospheric chemistry and dispersion of the pollutants concerned. Now there are concerns that many thousands of premature deaths may occur in the UK annually as a result of inhalation of particulates, and there is some evidence of links between air pollution and the incidence of asthma. Consequently both national and international legislation are constantly being tightened to reduce vehicle emissions, but much of the gains made in this respect are counteracted by increases in vehicle numbers.

4. Acid Rain and Ozone in Rural Areas

In the 1940s a new form of smog was observed for the first time in Los Angeles, which produced symptoms in humans such as eye and lung irritation and caused severe damage on vegetation. This was identified subsequently as being photochemical in origin, resulting from the action of bright sunlight on volatile organic compounds and nitrogen oxides, major sources of which are motor vehicle exhausts, under meteorological conditions with high temperatures and relatively still air. Later ozone *(03)* was identified as the most important damaging compound of the smog. Later, elevated levels of *03* were shown to occur over a very large part of the USA, with estimates in the mid-1980s indicating that this gas was causing $3 billion per year loss of yield of key agricultural crops. Unusually, *03* is a pollutant which occurs at higher levels in rural areas than in the cities, where its precursors emanate. Thus crops, forestry and native vegetation are particularly at risk.

No measurements had been made of tropospheric *03* in the UK before 1971, and indeed it was a widely held belief that it would not occur at pollutant levels under the prevailing meteorological conditions. When the first measurements were made it became clear that they were within the range found in parts of the USA where extensive damage to crops takes place. Subsequently it has been demonstrated that potentially damaging concentrations of 03 occur in summertime over most of Europe and experiments have shown clearly that the growth of a range of crop and other species can be impaired as a result. Thus as SO2 levels have fallen, it has become recognised that *03* is the most widespread and damaging gaseous pollutant in Europe as well as North America, so far as vegetation and rural areas are concerned.

From the beginning of the 1970s another widespread pollutant became increasingly recognised as representing a major and widespread environmental problem. This was acid precipitation, primarily derived from SO2 and nitrogen oxides being oxidised to sulphates and nitrates, respectively. The pH of pristine rain or snow is taken to be 5.6, which represents the acidity of distilled water in equilibrium with atmospheric carbon dioxide. However, studies around 30 years ago produced evidence that large areas of northern Europe received precipitation with a mean pH of 4.1 - 4.3, with episodes considerably more acid on occasions. This was associated with falling pH of rivers and lakes in affected areas where the soil was derived from slowly weathering rock like granite or gneiss, which provides minimal buffering of the acidity. In such places the falling pH and its associated release of toxic aluminium into solution resulted in severe adverse ecological effects, in particular the destruction of fish stocks. All the evidence pointed towards this acidification problem being caused largely by long distance transport of air pollution, much of it crossing international boundaries: the main areas affected were in southern Norway and Sweden, with Scotland and Wales identified later, the sources of the pollution largely being in the industrialised areas of central and western Europe, including the UK. This problem of transboundary air pollution resulted in massive international political disputes, lasting for many years before action was finally taken to address this issue.

In the early 1980s another widespread environmental problem emerged in both Europe and North America, which was popularly ascribed to acid precipitation. This was the appearance of a mysterious forest decline, which started in Europe in Germany. The symptoms of the decline included extensive yellowing and shedding of conifer needles, with die-back of secondary branches. The enormous scale of the decline and the large number of species affected led to the supposition that soil acidification resulting from acid deposition was the cause. Indeed, such acidification of sensitive soils has now been demonstrated as widespread in northern Europe. However, this is a complex issue which, unlike the causes of lake acidification and fish loss, remains largely unsolved. Claims in Germany some 15 years ago that total destruction of their forests would occur by the present time, have not remotely been justified. The fact that the decline also occurred in limestone areas, where acidification could not take place, raised serious doubts as to its cause and led to extensive research programmes attempting to elucidate the problem. Much of this work was aimed at determining the possible role of the other widespread pollutant - O_3 - in forest decline and evidence has been presented for this. At the present time the general view is that the decline is the result of many environmental factors, including both air pollution and natural stresses, as well as various forest management practices.

Yet another widespread cross boundary air pollution problem was identified in Europe in the mid 1980s. This was eutrophication of soils resulting from increased deposition of nitrogen. The latter is derived not only from nitrogen oxides, but also from ammonia and its derivatives, which originate from intensive livestock production. There is evidence that a large number of naturally low N ecosystems are being changed across Europe, with shifts in plant species composition in favour of those with a high N requirement and a concomitant loss of many low N species of high conservation value.

It can thus be seen that the last 30 years have seen the recognition of air pollution as not being merely a local issue, confined to cities and industrial areas, but as having regional and international scales, with pollutants derived from industrial, transport and agricultural sectors of the economy. This issue of transboundary air pollution has led to a range of protocols and directives being produced by the UN Economic Commission for Europe (UNECE) and the European Commission, respectively. Of particular significance here are the various protocols of the UNECE, which are resulting in the commitment of most European nations to make massive reductions in the emissions of SO_2, NO_x and volatile organic compounds over a fixed time-scale. These have in turn had enormous impacts on industry, not the least contributing to the decline in UK coal-mining, with indigenous sources being replaced by cheap low-S imported coal or else by sulphur-free natural gas.

5. The Global Dimension

In 1972 the book "The Limits to 'Growth" was published, which aroused a storm of controversy in that it predicted that human progress and economic growth would be brought to a halt in the relatively near future as a result of factors such as population growth, resource depletion (including food production) and global pollution. This was primarily the result of a massive computer modelling exercise, incorporating various sub-models. At the time the most criticised of these sub-models was that concerned with global pollution. In the event, nearly 30 years later, it is apparent that this is the issue which must be taken most seriously. Food production has kept pace with population growth, the rate of which, while unacceptably high, is nevertheless falling, and substitution and recycling have prevented depletion of mineral resources. However, there is effectively scientific consensus on the two major global air pollution problems viz, stratospheric ozone depletion and global warming. In the case of the former the demonstration of the adverse impacts of chlorine-containing gases on the stratosphere, with increased penetration of harmful ultra-violet radiation to the earth's surface, has resulted in unprecedented world-wide agreements to phase out the use of the gases concerned. The case of global warming is much more intractable, with a range of gases being involved in addition to CO_2. The latter is particularly problematical, resulting from extensive over-consumption in the developed world, while many developing countries seek to increase the standard of living of their population by rapid large-scale industrialisation, much of this being based on the use of coal as a fuel. Despite some moves being made towards reduction of greenhouse gas emissions, the political and economic interests ranged against such action leads to gloomy predictions over the ultimate consequences of global warming, such as sea-level rise, desertification and shifts in agricultural zones.

While the attention of politicians, the scientific community and the media is fixed on these truly global air pollution issues associated with greenhouse gases and stratospheric ozone depletion, far less attention is being paid to the "traditional" pollutants becoming serious environmental threats in much of the developing world, such that they can also be viewed essentially as "global". As mentioned previously the recognition in developed nations of the widespread serious damage caused by sulphur and nitrogen gases, photochemical oxidants and particulates has resulted in massive and costly actions to reduce emissions of the pollutants in question. Thus SO_2 emissions are predicted to fall from 22 to 14 and 15 to 14 million tonnes in Europe and the USA, respectively, from 2000 to 2010. Horrifyingly, emissions over the same period are predicted to rise from 34 to 48, 6.6 to 10.9, and 12.4 to 19.1 million tonnes in China,

India and elsewhere in Asia, respectively, largely due to increased coal burn. Already the same problems as have been recognised in Europe over the last 150 years are emerging in many developing countries, including serious deterioration of urban air quality and widespread occurrence of photochemical oxidants and acid rain. Not only is industry responsible for these problems, but so also are domestic sources and road transport, with the latter showing a massive increase of often poorly maintained old vehicles, with little or no emission controls.

Anybody visiting large cities in developing countries will notice the deterioration of air quality, resulting mainly from vehicle emissions, and this problem is now widespread. Photochemical smogs are a serious issue in many places, with Santiago and Mexico City being particularly bad in this respect. Such pollution is now the subject of many investigations on human health, with evidence of serious impacts on the urban poor, many of whom suffer from ill-health and malnutrition anyway. A very little studied further aspect of urban air pollution is the impacts that this may have on crop productivity in urban and peri-urban agriculture, which often play a major role in the nutrition of the poorer sections of the population. Current work in India, involving Imperial College indicates that loss of yield in such places may be very high.

Rural areas of some developing countries are also experiencing the air pollution problems recognised over the last 30 years as being widespread in Europe. Thus the pH of precipitation is now 4.25 in parts of southwest China, and this appears to be associated with a local forest decline. Model predictions indicate that this will become more widespread and that serious eutrophication problems will also appear in many developing countries. A recent modelling study has predicted that rising emissions of its precursors will result in O3 causing widespread and large reductions of yield of crops in China. In fact relatively little O3 monitoring is conducted in developing countries, particularly outside cities. However, the limited information available indicates that O3 concentrations occur which are potentially damaging to crops, including in Pakistan, Egypt, Mexico, Chile and South Africa. Despite the urgent need for most developing countries to increase their food production to feed rapidly growing populations, almost no attention has been paid to air pollution as representing a constraint on this, as opposed to more familiar stresses, such as salinity, drought and pest/pathogen attack. There is in fact limited but growing evidence that there may be major problems in this respect. Thus work at Imperial College has shown large reductions in rural or semi-rural areas in vegetable productivity in Egypt and soybean, rice and wheat yield in Pakistan, with all the evidence pointing towards O3 as being the prime cause.

6. Conclusions

It seems that air pollution, like the poor, "is always with us". No sooner than one problem is alleviated, then it seems that another appears. In some cases damage has been going on for a very long time, but has not been identified: indeed, it is known that acidification of sensitive lakes in Scotland started over 150 years ago. Over the last

30 years during which I have worked in air pollution research there has been a shift from the belief that SO_2 and smoke were the only significant pollutants to concerns over nitrogen oxides, O_3, acid rain, and, most recently, NH_3 volatile organic compounds and vehicle-derived particulates. Over this same period understanding has grown that air pollution has moved from being local to being regional, international and finally, global, in scale. It is interesting to speculate what will be the next areas of concern in the developed world and what new problems will be identified. In the developing world, it seems that, sadly, all the past problems of developed countries will become increasingly serious and present real threats to both the environment and human health. Truly, air pollution is an ever-changing threat.

THE CONSTRUCTION INDUSTRY - BUILDING ON THE PAST

Peter G. Fookes, F.I.M.M., F.R.S.A,. FGS F.R.Eng.
Emeritus Professor - Consulting Engineering Geologist
11A Edgar Road, Winchester, SO23 9SJ

1. The Construction Industry

Civil Engineers design and build engineering structures and are usually responsible for the structural aspects and the foundation design of buildings designed by Architects. The lecture concentrates on the interface between Engineering Geologists and Geomorphologists, and those Civil Engineers responsible for the foundations of structures and buildings. Major works such as dams, tunnels or harbours are not considered here.

1.1. The Civil Engineer's World

From earliest times, public works were undertaken by armies and their captives. When John Smeaton first described himself as a 'Civil Engineer' in 1768, he did more than differentiate himself and his colleagues from the Military Engineer, he identified a new vocation, the profession of civil engineering. Evolution went hand in hand with the new concept of the engineering profession and modem design and calculation based on experimental research began to take the place of old rules of thumb and empirical data. The theory of structures and study of materials advanced together as more and more refined stress analysis of structures and systematic testing was done. Today civil engineering is not solely confined to structural design, the designs of engineering works may require the application of theory from many fields, e.g. hydraulics, thermodynamics or seismology. Like geomorphology or geology, it is a living and growing science.

In the UK, current practice is for a largely theoretical three or four year civil engineering degree, followed by three or more years experience in industry at the end of which the graduate may submit designs and reports for professional examinations to become 'chartered'. The study of geology is also by a three year university course and in the last decade it has been possible for geologists to become chartered by virtue of their degree and post-degree experience, with submissions and interviews based somewhat on the civil engineering practice, but without a rigorous written examination.

1.2. Foundation Engineering

Figure 1 shows an interpretation of the relationship between civil engineering and the foundation aspects of the work. Soil Mechanicians are typically qualified civil engineers with a post-graduate qualification in soil mechanics, and Rock Mechanicians are typically civil or mining engineers. Engineering Geologists are usually geologists by virtue of their first degree, with experience or a post-graduate qualification in engineering geology.

No major project today is started without a feasibility study of various schemes to implement the project, leading to a recommended scheme, perhaps with alternatives. A preliminary site investigation is often part of the initial studies but once the scheme has been adopted, a more extensive investigation is usually imperative. The results of site investigations carried out during the design phase lead directly to the design of foundations and substructures of the project.

2. Foundations of Structures and Buildings

2.1. Principles of Foundation Engineering

The purpose of a foundation is to transfer the load of the structure to the ground, without causing it to respond with uneven or excessive movement. Most structures are supported on one of three principal types of foundations. The first type, commonly used for buildings, is spread foundations, (i.e. 'pads', below corners, or ends of ground beams; 'strips', generally below load bearing walls; or 'rafts', below whole buildings or structures). They function by spreading the load over a relatively large area of ground. The second is piles which are driven or bored into the ground, singly or in a group. Piles function by transferring the load of the building or structure into deeper or stronger ground. The third principal type is special foundations, mainly for structures, for example 'caissons'. All foundation types may be modified and combined to form the most suitable foundation for the ground conditions.

2.1.1. Foundation Failures

Most foundations settle because rocks and soils respond to the loads placed upon them. The intensity of loading that causes a failure to occur beneath a foundation is termed the bearing capacity of the ground. This capacity is governed by the fabric of the rocks and soils beneath a foundation and by the reaction of this fabric to any change in the effective stress - the pressure in a soil between the points of contact of the soil grains. Sometimes settlement results from other causes, such as the collapse of unstable soils above a concealed cavity, for example a solution hole in limestone or an abandoned or active mine. Some foundations rise because they are constructed on soils and rocks which expand when wetted, or by the formation of ice, or the crystallisation of gypsum. Foundations located on landslides may move laterally and vertically, usually at different speeds. Figure 2 gives examples of typical failure mechanisms beneath foundations.

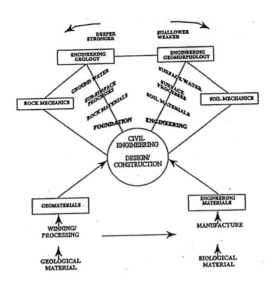

Figure 1 - A schematic relationship between civil engineering, geotechnology and geomaterials. (from Fookes, 1997)

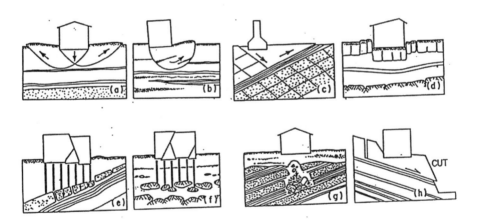

Figure 2 - Examples of failure mechanisms beneath foundations.
(a) and (b) are typical of sedimentary formations, (c) illustrates movement of rock (d) and (e) demonstrate the effect of over loading strong strata underlain by weak strata, (f) represents the problems that arise when boulders are mistaken for bed rock, (g) shows the upward growth of cavities that are not filled by bulking of the falling debris, and (h) records one of the difficulties of foundations on slopes. (from Blyth and De Freitas, 1984)

2.2. Characteristics of Soil and Rock Foundations

2.2.1. Foundations on 'Cohesive' Materials (i.e. Clays and Mudrocks)

Clays create the most difficult of the common founding conditions as they do not have the strength of rock and they can be consolidated by the building load. Consolidation settlement is caused by rearrangement of the soil particles which leads to a reduction in the void content of the soil. Where soils are saturated by groundwater the consolidation settlement must be accompanied by the expulsion of water from the soil, so that a long period of time is usually required for settlement to take place. The general approach to building on clays is to avoid loading the clay (e.g. transfer the load by piles, or spread the load on a raft), or to wait for the settlement to stop after the clay has been deliberately surcharged, i.e. overloaded. Consolidation of clay is accelerated by water loss during its working life and this is commonly exacerbated due to moisture extraction by tree roots or by pumped drainage. Extensive damage after the dry summers of 1976 and 1990 occurred on many houses situated, for example, on the Eocene London Clay, and the extensive Jurassic clays in southern and central England. Figures 3 and 4 illustrate settlement of clay, and subsidence caused by shrinkage. The famous Leaning Tower of Pisa was caused mainly by settlement due to compaction deformation of a soft clay layer some 11 to 22m below ground level.

2.2.2. Granular Soils, comprising Silt, Sands and/or Gravels

Silt, sands and gravels have no significant cohesion. Sands stand as steep slopes when wet due to negative pore pressure (sand castles rely on this) but will not stand so well when dry or saturated. The strength of such soils, both from a slope stability and a bearing capacity point of view, is derived from internal friction between the particles and varies with grading, packing, density and grain angularity. Settlement of such soils is small and rapid and takes place during construction. The bearing capacity of sandy soils may be improved for example, by dynamic consolidation (a large weight repeatedly dropped from a crane) or by vibro-compaction.

2.2.3. Rocks (Ranging from Weak, e.g. Weathered Chalk to Very Strong, e.g. Fresh Granite)

Sound rock is capable of bearing most normal engineering loads. Some forms of failure which can occur in unsound rock are, for example:

- Shear failure due to the imposed loading being greater than the rock strength.

- Rock failure into an underground cavity.

- Landsliding where the structure is too near the edge of a unstable slope.

- Compaction of porous rocks, due to loading being greater than the rock strength.

Ground improvement of fresh rock is rarely necessary or economic for structural foundations. However, weathered and weak rock near the surface is best removed or piled through. Occasionally grouting can be used to improve the strength of fissured rock or to fill cavities.

2.2.4. Special Conditions e.g. Buildings on Buried Voids

Buildings can subside where the ground material can be displaced into some sort of underground void. For example macro-voids are large cavities, e.g. solution caves in limestone and chalk (common in southern England), in salt or volcanic lavas, or mine cavities in any rocks of economic value (common in British Coal Measures). Failures under structural loading over underground cavities depend on the rock strength and fracturing, the cavity size and depth and the applied loads and stresses (see Figure 5). Mining subsidence produces foundation settlement and failures of various types. Old mines, whose records may have never existed or have long been lost, pose a risk for building construction. Micro-voids may occur in very porous deformable rocks, and in clays, peat and in some silts or sands, or in made ground.

3. Influence of climate zones on foundation characteristics of near surface soils and rocks

The current and past climatic zones have made important differences to the characteristics of near surface soils and rocks. World-wide changes of sea level during the Quaternary have also made problems (e.g. buried valleys) in near coast situations.

3.1. The Glacial Environment

Continental and valley glaciers are powerful agents of erosion and deposition and the important considerations for the engineer are the close relationships between the properties of the glacial sediments and those of the subjacent bedrock and location of former ice limits. Details of glacial land forms, glacial sediments and the effects on the ground vary significantly with climatic regime, the glacier size, the local geology and topography; in particular, variable tills and fluvio-glacial deposits are usually difficult to investigate and evaluate. Such conditions are especially important in Britain north of a line extending from west of Bristol to south of the Wash.

3.2. The Periglacial Environment

The importance of the freeze-thaw cycles related to periglacial conditions is in the disturbing effect they have on the ground. When periglacial processes occur in poorly drained fine-grained sediments, they are especially effective and near surface forms of disturbance (usually weakened or unstable ground) such as patterned ground, pingos and solifluxion lobes are common. Fossil periglacial features occur on about a third of the world's land surface including Britain (especially the chalk); and modern day periglacial conditions create active situations of ground movement during winter freezing and summer thawing, which can extensively damage foundations. The Alaska oil pipeline for example, has to be strongly protected against such movement.

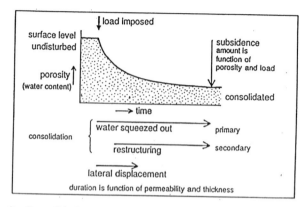

Figure 3 - Consolidation over time of clay under load (from Waltham, 1994)

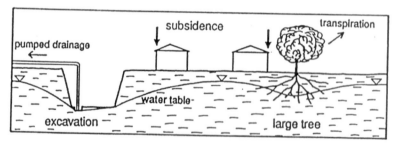

Figure 4 - Subsidence caused by shrinkage of clay on reduction of moisture content in the ground (from Waltham, 1994)

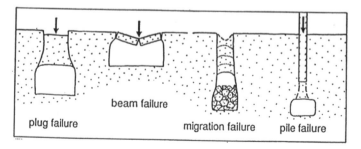

Figure 5 - Examples of failures overlying underground cavities. (from Waltham, 1994)

3.3. Hot Dryland Environment (i.e. 'Desert')

Such areas are characterised by a rain deficit and generally sparse vegetation. Again they cover at least a third of the world's land surface and vary greatly. Aeolian sediments (e.g. 'sand dunes' and 'loess') and aggressive salts are often expensive problems for engineering structures and flash floods, and sand and dust storms, hinder construction activities. Such effects are particularly important in much of the Middle East.

3.4. Wet Tropical Environment (i.e. the 'Tropics')

Engineering practice in tropical residual soils which are the product of hot wet tropical weathering, may be straightforward and can often be based successfully on local experience. However, some tropical residual soils frequently exhibit special engineering characteristics which differ from those found elsewhere and are generally a result of a porous structure or from the presence of certain clay minerals (e.g. smectites, andosols) in the genesis of the new soil. Such soils may have metastable characteristics and unusual properties such as high shrink and swell on drying and wetting, and construction of embankments may be severely hindered by their mobile behaviour.

Otherwise strong rock can be severely weakened by advanced stages of weathering prior to the rock developing into a residual soil. There is an engineering geology classification of weathered rock which has six categories, showing advancing degrees of weathering from the fresh rock until the sixth category which is the residual soil. Remnants of such soils and highly weathered rock can still be found in Britain especially south west England, parts of the Midlands and even parts of east Scotland. They are a legacy of sub-tropical weathering during the late Tertiary and in Inter-glacial periods during the Quaternary.

References

BLYTH, F.G.H. & DE FREITAS, M.H. 1984. *A Geology for Engineers*, Seventh Edition. Arnold, London.

FOOKES, P.G. 1997. The First Glossop Lecture. Geology for Engineers: the Geological Model, Prediction and Performance. *Quarterly Journal of Engineering Geology,* 30, 293-424.

WALTHAM, A.C. 1994. *Foundations of Engineering Geology*. Blackie, London.

THE OIL INDUSTRY AND THE WHIPPING BOY FOR A WORLD OUT OF CONTROL

Richard F. P. Hardman FGS CBE

Director Exploration Business, Amerada Hess Ltd, 33 Grosvenor Square, London, SW1X 7YH

Cheap energy, notably oil and to a lesser extent gas and coal, have brought the world unprecedented benefits in terms of living standards, life expectancy and quality of life. The burning of fossil fuels has given each of us the equivalent of 19 full time slaves without the need to house, cloth, feed and look after their general welfare. It was said that the Roman Empire was afloat on the sweat of the people that Rome had enslaved. Today we do not need to worry about the morality of slavery but nevertheless we do worry. Gradually increasing carbon dioxide levels linked to gradually increasing world ambient temperatures suggest that the activities of the human race may be destabilising the climate in an uncontrolled experiment. When looking round for someone to blame, the oil industry, because of its size, provides an obvious target especially since it supplies products which, when burned, yield carbon dioxide.

In the last 200 years the population of the globe has increased from 1 billion to 6 billion (Figure 1).

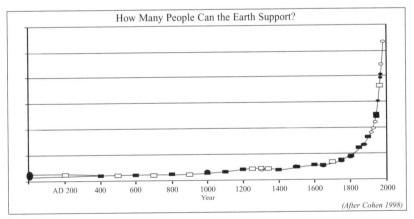

Figure 1: Estimated Human Population from AD1 to the Present

There seems to be a general correlation between improving living standards and a decrease in population growth. Cohen (1998) for instance, has shown that there is an intimate linkage between population, energy consumption, the environment and the prevailing culture. It is argued that the continued exploitation of fossil fuels provides the only practical way to raise living standards, stabilise population levels and develop economically attractive alternatives for generating energy from renewable sources such as wind, waves and sunlight. We must make the most of the opportunity since fossil fuels are finite resources and with the increasing population levels are are unlikely to meet demand over the next 20 to 30 years. Campbell (1997) for instance, suggests that oil production will peak before 2010 at approximately 80 million barrels/day and gas at 35 million barrels of oil equivalent/day some 10 years later. Ross (1998) concludes that by 2025 the world will require in addition to the equivalent of 50 million barrels from renewables, a minimum of 200 million barrels per day of oil equivalent energy to be delivered by coal, oil and gas (Figure 2). This is a 50% higher level of fossil fuel burn than today and, if Campbell is right, very difficult or impossible to achieve.

2025 Orchestrated Supply

	MMBDOE	Change vs. 1996
Coal	30	(35%)
Oil	70	0%
Gas	100	150%
Nuclear	40	208%
Hydro	7	75%
Renewables	53	N/A
Total	300	73%

1996-2025 Average Annual Growth

Energy	1.9%
Economy	3.5%
Average Oil Price	$15/B

Fear of climate change leads to global emissions controls

NOTE: DESPITE ATTEMPTS TO DECREASE FOSSIL FUEL BURN IT ACTUALLY INCREASES BY 15% FROM TODAY

Figure 2: One View of Energy Supply in 2025 *(After Ross 1998)*

We need to stop wringing our hands and take action now, as a recent paper in Nature by Parry et al (1998) shows (Figure 3), even if emissions were restricted to a greater extent than Kyoto, we will continue to experience global warming and climate change. We need to use the bounty of fossil fuels to ameliorate the worst effects of climate change, develop greater energy efficiency and new sources of energy. Finally, the real problem of the rapidly increasing global population can only be tackled by giving every person on the globe a stake in its future through a spread of democracy, a continued improvement in living standards, particularly in the poorest countries and a realisation that in this, as in everything, individual choices do matter.

Impacts Year 2050

EMISSIONS SCENARIO	WARMING °C REF 1961 - 1990	PEOPLE AT RISK (MILLIONS)		
		WATER	FLOODING	HUNGER
UNMITIGATED	1.39	1053	23	22
KYOTO*	1.33	1053	22	20
20% REDUCTION	1.22	909	21	17
30% REDUCTION	1.19	891	20	16

*Kyoto protocol signed by 38 countries accounting for 57% emissions

Figure 3: Global Warming Prediction and Possible Results *(After Parry et al 1998)*

References

Campbell, C.J. (1997) The Coming Oil Crisis, Multiscience Publishing Company and Petroconsultants SA, Brentwood England

Cohen, J. (1998) How Many People Can the Earth Support, Bull American Academy Arts and Sciences, Vol 51, March/April 1998 No 4

Parry, M., Arnell N., Houlme, M., Adapting to the Inevitable, Nature, Volume 395, Nicholls, R and Livermore, M. (1998), 22 October 1998

Ross, C.E. H. (1998) Industry Outlook Report - Different Oil Industries for Different Futures, PRISM, Arthur D Little Q4/98

EVOLUTION OF THE OIL INDUSTRY — ITS IMPORTANCE TO THE ROLE OF THE PETROLEUM GEOLOGIST

Malcolm Brown FGS

B G International, 100 Thames Valley Park, Reading, RG6 1PT

From its inception in the 1880s the oil industry has had a turbulent history. From the days of Rockefeller and the break up of Standard Oil, through the giant Middle East discoveries in the 1930s and 1940s and subsequent nationalisation, the fortunes of the industry have been very cyclical in nature. The oil crises of the 1970s led to prices escalating to over $30/barrel, which accelerated the exploration and development of major reserves in new basins such as the North Sea. Oil prices, however, are notoriously variable, due mainly to the influence and unpredictability of OPEC, leading to dramatic price drops and subsequent industry downsizing, such as in 1986. In the last year, for example, oil prices have varied between $9 and $23 per barrel, and even the latter is historically low in real terms.

Mergers of oil majors have recently occurred on a scale that would have been unthinkable a year or two ago and 'downsizing' is the norm. The majors are progressively exiting from mature provinces that are unable to produce the reserves needed to replace production at a competitive cost. This includes much of the North Sea, one of the new provinces of thirty years ago, now moving into a new phase where smaller independents are playing an increasingly important role.

The world views the oil industry with considerable suspicion, disliking its large profits, ignorant of the risks and technical challenges. The industry has only itself to blame for mismanaging its image at times, but profits made by oil companies are often portrayed as more obscene than those made by banks and IT companies! This unpopularity is largely driven by the fact that most people's contact with oil companies is at the petrol pump. This is an emotive subject and one in which the price bears no relationship to the cost of production, the vast majority being tax. The public is generally unaware that, despite the application of leading edge technologies, finding hydrocarbons is still a high risk business with, on average, four out of five exploration wells being dry. There is also a limited knowledge of the benefits to daily life provided by the oil industry that turn up in a huge array of consumer goods. They are also unaware that the people responsible for this critical first step of creating wealth both for shareholders and also the tax paying population, are geologists.

The objective of this talk is to look at the human side of this industry. I would like to look at the future prospects of the petroleum geologist and geophysicist, not just the ones currently employed but as a profession. This is not a Luddite view of progress versus the 'good old days', but a look at the evolving world and its impact on some remarkable scientists whose technical achievements are rarely understood.

I have chosen three themes to illustrate the changes that impact the petroleum geologist.

- The potential domination by very large oil companies created by mergers to form 'super majors'.
- The increase in outsourcing of geological work by oil companies.
- The developments in technology, which are radically changing the way in which geologists work.

2. A future domination by 'super majors'?

The recent spate of mergers (Exxon-Mobil, BP-Amoco-Arco), raises the question of whether there is a role for the smaller company and consequently the geologists employed there. Mergers invariably lead to a shakeout of 'non core' assets that don't fit the strategy of the new company. These often form the ideal 'starter pack' for a new generation of small oil companies that restart the cycle. Is this simply part of a habitual cycle or is the industry changing fundamentally?

In the days of Standard Oil size did matter, access to the cheapest reserves and supply routes led to its domination. At present the 'super majors' dwarf most other oil companies. They are, however small compared to the other giants of the industry, the National Oil Companies (NOCs) of the major OPEC oil producers, Saudi Arabia, Iran, Iraq, Mexico, Venezuela etc. The oil and gas reserves of the NOCs are five-to-ten fold those of the major oil companies and generally are cheaper reserves to produce. Greater access to the vast low cost reserves of OPEC is the dream of all oil companies. In the past the income of the OPEC states was sufficiently large that no external funding was required. However, lower oil prices and burgeoning social and infrastructure costs have led to a need to obtain foreign investment funds for oil and gas developments. There is a natural reluctance within the countries to do this, leading to a variety of 'limited access' opportunities. Examples of these are the 'buy back' contracts in Iran, the 'apertura', or opening of the industry, in Venezuela and the ending of the Petrobras monopoly in Brazil.

A combination of global politics and the reluctance to 'sell the nation's birthright' has restricted the penetration of the super majors into these large low cost reserves to date. If there is a significant increase in access, such a change could be dramatic. The great efficiency gains the industry has achieved during low oil price periods could be applied to the large, low cost OPEC reserves, and this would undercut all other reserves. The majors could withdraw from higher cost production elsewhere, concentrating on maximum returns. Therefore the role of both the independent and the governments of the higher cost, mature provinces would be fundamentally changed. This would potentially create the next major step in the evolution of the oil industry, bringing a fundamental change to the market.

If this happened there would be a significant and negative impact on the role of the petroleum geologist. Many fewer geologists would be needed as an increasing amount of the world's supply would come from a limited number of fields and countries.

3. Outsourcing

The second theme is a change in where the work gets done. Thirty years ago oil companies would have directly employed all aspects of the geological work carried out in the search for oil and gas. This would have included fieldwork, well site geology, biostratigraphy, geochemistry, core analysis, structural geology as well as prospect generation. On the geophysical side, acquisition and processing of seismic, gravity and magnetic data was also routinely conducted by oil company staff. Seismic was one of the earlier parts of the business to be outsourced, partly due to its specialised nature. In recent years the industry has continued to reduce the range of core skills that it believes are necessary to keep 'in house'. This has been due to continual pressure to reduce overhead costs and therefore head count. This does not mean the skills are no longer needed, instead these are 'bought in' from contractors or consultants. This may have a number of benefits, it may simply be more cost efficient, alternatively, it may provide access to a better service or knowledge due to the contractor specialising in this area for a number of companies. The question every company must ask is what are their core skills - what gives them a competitive advantage? This may vary across the industry, some companies may feel their edge is in exploration or development, for others it may be minimising operating costs. Some companies have an ability to bring together gas reserves and market, creating a 'gas chain'. Whichever it is it will dictate the skills that the company must control and develop, whilst taking advantage of a flourishing external market for others.

Therefore in the new world you may play a key role in the oil industry without ever working for an oil company!

4. Developments in Technology

As in many disciplines the step change in the way in which geologists work has been enabled by huge improvements in computing power. The key step is the increasing use of 3D seismic to create a data cube that can then be manipulated extensively. Examples of this include:

- Visualisation techniques that allow the identification of seismic data with specified attributes, e.g. bright amplitudes indicating presence of gas, from a large data volume. This can save much time in focussing on the areas of interest and when calibrated with well data allows more accurate reservoir models to be created faster. This in turn may reduce the number of appraisal wells and therefore time to production.

- Automatic electric log and seismic interpretation tools via neural nets and rule based algorithms will allow evaluation 'real-time'. Results of the integration of these tools, tying both the vertical interpretation from logs with lateral predictions using seismic, can be converted to predictions of reservoir facies and properties.

- 3D or 4D basin modelling to reduce risk by more accurate understanding and prediction of the hydrocarbon system prior to drilling.

- Forward geological modelling by means of 'intelligent software', that can simulate geological depositional and structural processes. When integrated with basin or reservoir simulation tools this will allow a more accurate understanding of the areas between well or outcrop control and potentially highlight new plays.

- Geologists will need to understand the principles on which these techniques are based. As a consequence, however, he or she should be able to spend more time evaluating the results rather than doing the interpretation.

5. Conclusions

One thing that has not changed in the industry is risk. It was a risky and geologically poorly understood business in Rockefeller's days. Our understanding of geology has developed over the years but the exploration targets are deeper, hotter or more complex than before. The easy targets (if they ever existed!) have gone. Although there have been great improvements in drilling technology it is still an expensive business. Well costs can exceed $30m each in many provinces and the chance of the well being successful is still only a one in ten chance in frontier areas. Improving this chance of success relies on the skill, knowledge and judgement of the geologist.

Oil and gas are both essential commodities at the start of the new millennium, possibly even more so than a century ago. The geologist's role will continue to develop with technological advance and the numbers required will evolve with the business environment. Ultimately, oil and gas is only found by geologists - no one else, their role in the oil industry continues to be essential and it is important this contribution of our profession to society is recognised.

COAL MINE METHANE - A FUEL FOR THE FUTURE

Cameron Davies FGS

Coalgas Plc. c/o 102 Warwick Park, Tunbridge Wells, Kent TN2 5EN

1. Introduction

Coal mine methane has recently been recognised as one of the major components of anthropogenic greenhouse gas emissions to atmosphere. Its global warming effect is estimated by the International Panel on Climate Change as being 58 times that of carbon dioxide. The US Environmental Protection Agency estimates that coal mine methane emissions in the UK, were approximately 1 billion cubic metres per year in 1990. These emissions could be reduced by more than 55 percent by 2010 as a result of the down turn in the coal industry, recovery of methane from abandoned coal mines and coalbed methane drilling. This would be the equivalent of removing approximately 2 million cars from the road by the end of this period.

Coal mine methane, the major component of mine gas, was traditionally viewed by mining companies as a hazardous waste product which was expensive to remove from operating mines in order to keep them safe. When the British coal industry was nationalised in 1947, there were more than 947 operating deep coal mines, whereas there are now only 15. Thus, country-wide there are hundreds of abandoned mines leaking methane to atmosphere via shaft vents, relief boreholes and geological faults and fissures.

Coalgas Plc, formed in 1994 to exploit methane being vented to atmosphere from abandoned coal mines, estimates that harnessing this gas for use as fuel could eliminate greenhouse emissions equivalent to millions of tonnes per annum of carbon dioxide and in doing so reduce its global warming effect by more than 95%.

In the first quarter of 1999, Coalgas brought mine gas extraction plants on stream at two abandoned collieries in the East Midlands. The first, at Markham vent in Derbyshire, supplies mine gas via a pipeline to Coalite and the second, at Steetley in Nottinghamshire, fuels a power station owned by Independent Energy (UK) Ltd. These two plants are already reducing annual emissions by more than 200,000 tonnes of carbon dioxide equivalent per annum and this should more than double when both projects are operating at full capacity. A third plant at Shirebrook in Derbyshire began generation in the first quarter 2000.

Coalgas is planning additional projects for 2000 at the abandoned Wheldale and Allerton Bywater mines in Yorkshire and at Bickershaw in Lancashire which could quadruple the total savings.

The company believes that coal mine methane, an indigenous energy resource located in the industrial heart of the UK, should be classed as "green" in the same way as landfill gas because it provides a proven route to immediate reductions in UK greenhouse gas emissions. Coalgas technology is reliable, safe, available now and generates emissions credits at costs lower than those of other renewables. The Government should therefore recognise that this niche gas source has an important role to play in providing balance in the UK's energy supply market.

In addition, the export potential of this environmentally friendly technology and related know-how is immense as many countries world-wide are moving to fewer but more efficient deep mines and abandoning large numbers of gassy coal mines.

2. Coal Mine Methane

Coal gas or firedamp, as it used to be known, consists mainly of methane mixed with carbon dioxide and nitrogen. The gas is hazardous to men and operations when released by mining operations. In order to keep working mines safe, the gas is removed in ventilation air or if concentrations are too high, it is extracted via methane drainage systems. In the past, British Coal either vented this operating mine gas to atmosphere or in some cases used it as fuel for hot water boilers or on-site electricity generation. Methane extracted from two abandoned mines in South Wales and Lancashire was used as a fuel on a small scale during the sixties and seventies.

The results of these projects and the success of the Methamine extraction plant in France gave strong evidence that abandoned mines contain large quantities of mine gas which could be captured and used as fuel. In the UK, abandoned mine gas was for many years considered neither as a surface hazard nor a significant contributor to greenhouse gas emissions. However, incidents such as the discovery of high concentrations of methane in houses at Arkwright, Derbyshire and the subsequent demolition and removal of the village, have raised official and public awareness that gas leaking from abandoned coal mines can be a significant surface hazard. Coalgas operating gas production plants at Steetley, Markham and Shirebrook have proved that this hazard can be turned into a commercial energy source.

3. History

Before the First World War, the UK coal mining industry was one of the largest in the world, employing over 1 million people. With the closure of over 900 mines after nationalisation, tens of thousands of jobs were lost but 75% of the original coal remained unextracted and the remaining coal reserves contain large reserves of adsorbed methane. Under certain conditions this gas desorbs i.e. is released from the surface of the coal, filling the old mine workings and surrounding fractured strata to form an underground gasometer.

Some abandoned mines were capped and fitted with vent pipes by British Coal to prevent the build up of underground pressure and protect against methane seeping from old workings into houses, drains and sewers. Other deep mine shafts were filled and sealed to cut off migration routes to surface of this hazardous gas. Coalgas has gathered information from mining archives which indicates that there are at least 250 abandoned mines within its licence areas which may be emitting several million tonnes of CO2 equivalent per annum. Coalgas is currently planning to capture and sell coal mine methane from 40 of these sites over the next 5 years.

4. Coalgas Operations

Coalgas has developed technology to capture and commercialise the waste gas venting from abandoned coal mines and reduce its greenhouse effect by 95%. The company acquired a widespread acreage portfolio from the DTI covering UK coalfields and has acquired a unique knowledge of abandoned mine gas behaviour. Its R & D programmes have resulted in the Markham and Steetley gas extraction plants being brought on stream in the first quarter of 1999 with sales of metered gas to industrial end users.

At Markham (Plate 1a & 1b), mine gas is extracted from vents which access the old workings via the 437 metre deep Number 3 shaft. The extracted gas is delivered to the customer via a pipeline which passes beneath colliery spoil heaps reprofiled by Derbyshire County Council ready for the industrial park development. The gas is metered at the exit flange before delivery to the customer site where it is used as burner tip fuel.

At Steetley (Plate 1c & 1d), a similar modular extraction system has been connected to the vent on Number 1 Shaft. The gas is delivered to an on-site power station which exports electricity to its customers via an EME sub-station.

Plate 1. Abandoned Mines Sites

1a - Markham Vent   Before

1b - Markham Vent   After

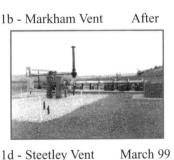

1c - Steetley Vent   Sept. 98

1d - Steetley Vent   March 99

5. Future Developments

In addition to the Shirebrook plant which began to generate 95MW of electricity earlier in the year. Coalgas has identified more than 280 abandoned deep coal mines within its licence areas, some of which are vented and others which will require gas drainage boreholes drilled into the old workings to access the reserves. The company is currently investigating the commercial potential of these sites by monitoring gas flow rates, reservoir pressures, methane purity, water levels and other relevant factors using Coalgas developed data loggers. The company is also co-operating with power generators on the feasibility of combined heat and power plants in future green energy parks and also community based district heating schemes.

6. Environmental and Community Benefits

Methane has a global warming potential 58 times greater than that of carbon dioxide. Coalgas's extraction plants remove this hazardous waste gas from the atmosphere and use it as a sustainable, local energy resource. The increasing numbers of plants should contribute significantly to reducing the UK's output of greenhouse gases. In addition, abandoned mine gas extraction projects bring jobs into economically deprived mining communities and help kick start economic regeneration of derelict mine sites.

7. Climate Change Levy

Coalgas believes that mine gas, a newly recognised, sustainable source of energy should be treated in the same way as renewable energy for the following reasons:

i) Mine gas capture reduces UK greenhouse gas emissions
ii) Reserves of gas could extend for 50 years or more
iii) Coal, the primary energy source remains untouched
iv) Exploitation eliminates a local hazard cf. Arkwright
v) It is a local energy source in derelict industrial zones
vi) Ideal for embedded power generation

8. Conclusion

Coalgas abandoned mine gas extraction technology has shown that a hazardous greenhouse gas can be profitably converted into fuel for power generation and burner tip use.

The company's gas production plants are already extracting and selling this green energy to end users and in doing so making significant reductions in the UK's greenhouse gas emissions.

"NEEDED NEW EARTH RESOURCE TECHNOLOGIES, NEW GEO-ETHICS FOR THE 21ST CENTURY"

William S. Fyfe FRS
Dept. of Earth Sciences, University of Western Ontario,
London, Ontario, Canada N6A 5B7

1. Introduction

It is interesting to look back at the classic work on the biosphere by Vladimir Vernadsky. In 1926 he wrote about a new geological era which he termed the psychozoic era. He recognised that mankind would be a new and powerful entity able to transform the planet. Today there is no doubt about this prediction. Our actions have changed the atmosphere, the biosphere, the hydrosphere and the land surface. Since the famous Bruntland Report of 1987, Our Common Future, we frequently use the term sustainable development. Will the actions of our generation improve the quality of life for future generations? I think the situation was nicely summarised by Sir Crispin Tickell in his British Association lecture of 1993.

"I was recently asked if I was an optimist or a pessimist. The best answer was given by someone else. He said that he had optimism of the intellect but pessimism of the will. In short we have most of the means for coping with the problems we face, but are distinctly short on our readiness to use them. It is never easy to bring the long term into the short term. Our leaders, whether in politics or business, rarely have a time horizon of more than five years."

The 20th Century has been remarkable in terms of the development of *Homo sapiens*. Two thousand years ago the human population has been estimated at about 300 million. It then took 1700 years to double the population; social conflict, disease and famine controlled the global population. Then came the birth of modern science and technology and the beginning of new knowledge about our planet. The giants of the period around 1800 (from Lyell to Darwin to Einstein) opened new visions including the understanding of atoms and energy and planetary systems. We now live in the age of observation on all scales. The thoughtless application of the new knowledge led to the present population explosion. But as has been noted recently by many people (see the Economist, September 11, 1999) during these developments, by war and government actions over 200 million people have been killed, almost the world population 2000 years ago.

When we examine our life support systems, our quality of life, major components include:

- Adequate, high quality food

- Adequate, high quality water

- Clean air to breathe

- Adequate energy for all our needs

- Materials for all our needs from construction to computers

When we examine such components, it is obvious that all involve our understanding of the Earth-Sun system. Our mineral resources essentially all come from the outer few kilometres of the solid earth. Advanced societies use about 20 tonnes of rock-derived materials per person, per year. For a population of 10 billion living at an advanced quality of life, this means 2×10^{14} kg of rock per year, or almost 100 km3 per year. This quantity exceeds the volume of all the volcanism on the planet, on land and submarine, by an order of magnitude. Human actions are now a major component of the processes that modify the planet's surface.

But today it is clear that we must improve quality control in the source of our materials. We all like to find gold ore. But do we discuss the components frequently associated with the gold, components like lead, arsenic. A recent report in Harper's Magazine, October 1999, illustrates the situation. The report, Tarnished Gold, discusses the recent goldmining in Papua New Guinea where cyanide, arsenic, lead, pollution has killed all life in some rivers and the developments have led to local conflicts killing 15,000 people.

As the world becomes crowded, the land surface becomes more precious. First we must manage quality, the key to recycling technologies. We can develop new mining extraction technologies. The new knowledge of the deep biosphere could lead to in situ metal solutions as with sulphide oxidizing bacteria. Certain algal species accumulate gold and elements like arsenic. And as recent work in New Zealand shows, some trees are very efficient in accumulating gold. But of vast future importance are the spectacular new discoveries of metal deposits on the sea floor near ocean ridges, subduction zones and even the quiet ocean floor. And there is vast potential to couple geothermal energy use with metal extraction.

The modern literature abounds with reports of the problems of water supply in a host of nations. At the present time we manipulate almost 40% of the reliable, usable, water on the continents. In a host of nations, careless irrigation technologies have led to salinization. In a host of nations, too much use of groundwater is lowering the water table and producing more saline waters. And problems like arsenic pollution, fluorine pollution are becoming catastrophic. We have recently been working on the water-arsenic problem and found that it is not difficult to remove arsenic by absorption on sulphide minerals or by using sulphate reducing bacteria or certain algal species. But a new problem arises. Where do we put the wastes?

The new world data are mindboggling. In 1950, there were just over 5,000 large river dams. In 1985 this number had reached over 30,000! Will any rivers flow to the ocean freely in 2050? What will be the influence on ocean biomass, ocean currents, climate?

Our present energy technologies are not sustainable. Today, most of the world's energy comes from burning oil, gas, coal. The technology of burning carbon has never changed - add air - burn - exhaust to the atmosphere. We have changed the atmosphere and the climate. The world is divided into those who waste energy led by nations like the U.S.A. and Canada, those who are trying to conserve, Europe and Japan, and many who need more energy. If all the people of 2050 produced greenhouse gases like certain advanced nations, our planet would become like Venus.

Can we provide adequate clean energy for 10 billion people? This is one of the greatest, most urgent questions for science and technology. There is no doubt that ultimately we must go to solar energy and there are spectacular new developments as with the surface-catalyzed photo-dissociation of water to produce hydrogen and oxygen, almost the perfect fuel. Another area of great interest involves the possible disposal of combustion gases underground or in the deep oceans. But all these technologies require new materials, new knowledge. Again we have seen careless use of geo-materials like coal. There are coals rich in halogens, rich in arsenic and many other dangerous species. And where will we isolate the nuclear wastes for a million years? This is a classic case of international responsibility and the need for international cooperation. It has only been in recent years that we have become truly concerned with the management of wastes of all types, solid, liquid, gas, which result from human activities. As the land surface and water become more precious, new systems must be developed and all must involve the earth sciences.

A new term used more frequently by the United Nations and similar organisations is "food security". At the core of food production is soil, water, climate. Global soil erosion is in many nations catastrophic with almost 1% of topsoil being lost every year. Recently we have shown that when soils erode by wind and water, the fine clay minerals are lost, reducing capacity of the soil to retain water, and more irrigation is needed. Recent work has shown vast areas of soil pollution, some resulting from lack of quality control of fertiliser minerals. Again the earth sciences must be more involved in the mineralogy, the geo-microbiology, the total geochemistry needed for soil remediation.

In conclusion, world data are clear. In nations where the quality of life, the quality of the environment is improving, education for all people is the priority. All people must understand their life support systems. We have the knowledge to solve most of our problems, but we must develop new systems, new teams, where we integrate the expertise from all science, engineering and particularly from economics. I will use examples in my lecture to show that clean technology is always good economics.

And it is also clear that there is need for new global ethics in the use of our planet. For example, when European and North American companies develop mineral resources and agricultural resources abroad, they must use technologies as they would in their own nation.

CONSERVING THE PAST TO CHANGE THE FUTURE

Colin Prosser PhD and Jonathan Larwood PhD

English Nature, Northminster House, Peterborough PE1 1UA

1. Introduction

Throughout our history, mankind has utilised and exploited the natural environment, whether as a source of food or building material, or to provide fuels or mineral resources to support our evolving industries and society. Never before, however, has the impact of mankind on our planet been so high on the social and political agenda. Demands by society for more housing, more roads, more drinking water and more food are producing an increasingly stressed environment in which the impact of development, water abstraction, production of waste and the pollution of water and air have placed the fate of our environment high into the global political arena.

To help counter these concerns, the concept of 'sustainable development' was firmly established at the Rio Earth Summit in 1992. This concept, now widely adopted across the World, requires that economic development should take full account not only of the costs of resource consumption, waste production and pollution, but also of the wider impact on the environment. In the UK, sustainable development forms a common thread through Government policy, its importance and the Government's vision for how it will be delivered, is outlined in the Government's Sustainable Development strategy 'A better quality of life' (1999). This emphasises the value of integrating the social, environmental and economic strands of human activity, with the wise use of natural resources being central to this.

To many the diversity and quality of our wildlife has long been seen as a measure of the health of our environment. If, at least, we can maintain our level of biodiversity then we can demonstrate that sustainable development is being achieved. In a step towards conserving our biodiversity, Biodiversity Action Plans have been introduced. Everyone from conservationist through to business is expected to play their part in meeting these biodiversity conservation targets and in helping to achieve a sustainable future for our environment.

But where, you may ask, does geology sit within all of this? We, as Earth scientists, may fully appreciate the value of our Earth heritage both in understanding our changing planet and in resource management, but is the conservation of our Earth heritage part of the growing environmental awareness in the minds of the politicians and the public? What can we do to ensure our Earth heritage is safe from increasing development and landfill, how can we increase its value to society? And what contribution can we, as Earth scientists make to the political and social decision making required to ensure that generations to come have a future worth waiting for?

2. Conserving the past

In Great Britain, Earth heritage conservation has always been a core element of nature conservation, and is central to the work of the statutory conservation agencies. We in the UK, are amongst the most experienced nations, in terms of managing and conserving our Earth heritage resource. We have already selected sites of national importance for their Earth heritage on a Great Britain basis through the Geological Conservation Review (GCR) and in England these sites are now largely protected under the Wildlife and Countryside Act as Sites of Special Scientific Interest (SSSI). Furthermore, the last few years has seen the rise of voluntary Earth heritage conservation on a local scale. The Regionally Important Geological/Geomorphological Sites (RIGS) movement has added the conservation of hundreds of new sites to the conservation portfolio. Thus, we have sites identified and protected within the planning system, and alongside this have developed through fifty years experience, a clear understanding of how to manage this resource, whether an eroding coast, a working quarry or a roadside cutting.

Earth heritage sites are still threatened, however, by physical pressures such as coastal protection, landfill, development and irresponsible collecting but perhaps the greatest threat is that of ignorance. Whether a key decision maker, policy formulator or a member of the general public, it is the lack of understanding of the importance of our Earth heritage resource that poses the greatest and longest term threat to its future.

English Nature is now increasingly directing its efforts towards the management of sites, raising awareness of their value and advocating how they should be managed in the long-term. Simple physical improvement of Earth heritage sites, whether through removal of concealing vegetation, rubbish or scree, provision of straight forward interpretation or the promotion of sustainable management practices such as responsible fossil collecting, will all add to a greater appreciation of our Earth heritage resource. Equally, we continue to raise awareness of the need to conserve our Earth heritage resource with decision makers in Government, the minerals industry and local authorities. If we are to succeed, however, more needs to be done by all Earth scientists.

Society will only see the need to conserve our Earth heritage resource if it places a value on it, and will only value it if they understand the resource and its relevance to them. This will only happen if we as Earth scientists, continue to explain our subject in exciting and relevant ways. We need to do for rocks and fossils what the RSPB has done for birds, or perhaps what David Attenborough has done for 'Life on Earth'. We need to use dinosaurs, evolution, volcanoes, earthquakes and building stones. We need to demonstrate the interdependence of geology, landscape, habitats, species and people to make the subject more relevant and understood. (Figure 1)

Figure 1 - Liassic limestones exposed on the foreshore of Blue Anchor to Lilstock Coast SSSI, Somerset - the coming together of geology, landscape, and modern habitats and species.

(Photograph: Peter Wakely)

3. Changing our future

Can understanding and conserving our Earth heritage change the future of our environment?

Our Earth heritage is important in its own right but it can also be seen to be important for what it tells us about the dynamic nature of our environment and therefore what the future may hold in store for us. What greater incentive could there be for us to conserve our Earth heritage.

How many times have climates changed, how many times have sea levels risen and fallen and how many species have become extinct? Evidence for all this change is locked up in the rocks that surround us. It is also the diversity of these rocks and the evolution of our landscape over time that underpins the diversity of our habitats and wildlife. This is all part of our Earth heritage resource, and understanding this, provides a far better context for formulating planning policies that will help to deliver sustainable development and general nature conservation in its broadest sense. For example:

- Planning for climate change. The geological record shows climate change and the consequent geographical shift of habitat and species. What can this tell us about the impact of changing climate today? What does this mean for the conservation of habitats and species susceptible to climate change? Why do we try to hang on to habitats and species in areas where changing climate has made them no longer viable ? And what decisions should we make to manage our environment in the light of the inevitable?

- Planning for sea level rise. Marine rocks present across central England show that we cannot stop the sea. Understanding that sea levels will rise and that coastlines will move is essential in the formulation of policies geared to move development away from eroding coasts and shift from defending coastlines with concrete, to a softer and more natural approach that allows some managed realignment.

- Planning for changing biodiversity. The geological record shows us that extinction is normal. Geologically we have background extinction rates against which enhanced extinction, culminating in mass extinction, can be measured. We must appreciate that some loss in biodiversity will occur, this loss could be local, regional or even global. We must be sure we understand and manage natural losses against those caused by human activity.

- Planning mineral extraction. Only by understanding the extent of our mineral resources can we formulate sustainable policies for theft usage and only by under standing the impact of extraction on habitats and wildlife can these policies be truly sustainable. The potential gains for conservation of both biodiversity and our Earth heritage, arising from appropriate quarry restoration, also need to be fully realised.

- Understanding active processes. Understanding modern sedimentary processes is essential to understanding how the environment may change in response to our intervention. This understanding must inform the development of policies in areas such as coastal management, water abstraction and management, or quarrying. (Figure 2)

Figure 2 - Woodeaton Quarry SSSI provides one of the most complete Bathonian sections in Oxfordshire - quarrying provides an opportunity now to examine these sections and approporaite restoration a long term future for geology.

(Photograph: Peter Wakely)

It is essential that we sift out the impact of natural change against the impact of human activity on the environment, whether through the burning of fossil fuels, pollution of water or destruction of habitat. The geological record, our Earth heritage resource, is a key to understanding natural change and its impact. Understanding this will allow the focus to be placed on ameliorating the impact of humans on the environment balancing this against the effects of an ever evolving environment.

4. Conclusion

'The past is the key to the future' has become central to English Nature's direction in Earth heritage conservation. Studying and understanding our Earth heritage resource can help us change the future of our society and of the environment in which we live. To achieve this understanding of our geological past, and gain an insight into the future, we need to ensure we conserve the resource in the first place. Our Earth heritage provides us with a crystal ball, and if we all play our part and make it work for society, its long-term conservation will be guaranteed.

DINOSAUR RESEARCH. 160 YEARS OF PROGRESS?

David Norman FGS

Sedgwick Museum, University of Cambridge, Downing Street, CB2 3EQ

The early remains of dinosaurs were decidedly fragmentary, and enigmatic: strange large teeth and isolated bones. These were studied scientifically during the first three decades of the nineteenth century by such luminaries as Georges Cuvier (Paris), William Buckland (Oxford) and Gideon Mantell (A physician based at Lewes in Sussex). Such remains were given formal scientific names and were regarded, largely on the advice of Cuvier, as providing evidence of a time in the Earth's distant past when giant land reptiles had lived. Such discoveries were complemented by equally startling finds of giant fossil marine reptiles: mosasaurs, plesiosaurs and ichthyosaurs. These decades very much brought to light the amazing scientific treasures that could be quarried from the Earth and used to explore, or begin to understand, deep prehistoric time. Thus the giant fossil land reptiles (later to become dinosaurs) were considered to be gigantic versions of the reptiles known today - essentially lizard or crocodile-like in their proportions.

Dinosaurs, as a wholly distinct group of fossil organisms, were invented by Professor Richard Owen FRS (Owen, 1842). It has been shown by Professor Hugh Torrens (Torrens, 1992) that Owen invented this name while he was editing, and substantially re-writing, the lengthy second report which completed his survey of the then known British Fossil Reptiles. A draft of this report formed the substance of a lecture to the 11th meeting of the British Association for the Advancement of Science held at Plymouth in 1841. It has been recounted that Owen took some two and a half hours to deliver the report, and would no-doubt have tested the endurance of even the most enthusiastic and determined of conference-goers. The 140 page report is nothing if not comprehensive but, sadly, lacked any illustrations whatsoever; this probably lent to these his dinosaurs something of the mystic quality that characterised some of Owen's writings. Given that dinosaurs were only then known from the scrappiest of material (a few enigmatic bones and teeth), it is quite remarkable that Owen was able to tease apart, from the bewildering variety of fossil reptiles that had been discovered up to that time, what was to prove to be such an important and distinctive group of extinct animals.

It took, however, another twelve years for dinosaurs to arouse significant public attention, but this was very dramatic indeed. In 1854 dinosaurs and many other prehistoric animals (ichthyosaurs, plesiosaurs, dicynodonts, etc.) were feted as a significant and imaginative part of the celebrations surrounding the re-opening of Sir Joseph Paxton's enormous Crystal Palace (originally erected as a temporary building on Hyde Park) in parklands at Sydenham (McCarthy and Gilbert, 1994). The landscaped palace grounds were adorned by concrete models of these ancient monsters set in a geological garden; this was to have a combined theatrical and educational appeal. The models were set in a series of geological landscapes each representing distinctive periods of past time and their appropriate fossil fauna and this was explained in a detailed guidebook (Owen, 1854). Considerable publicity was generated during the building of these prehistoric creatures by the Crystal Palace Company and the flamboyant sculptor Benjamin Waterhouse Hawkins, culminating in a well-publicised celebratory New Year's Eve dinner (1853/4 - see the December and January issues of the London Illustrated News) held inside the mould of the dinosaur *Iguanodon*. As a result tens of thousands of people came to view the prehistoric monsters and gained a strong visual and physical impression of the way in which scientific research had led to the unearthing of these truly remarkable creatures that had lain, unsuspected, under the ground. The social impact of these models is hard to imagine today, but the fact that dinosaur names, such as *Megalosaurus*, made their way into the almost soap-opera-like novels of Charles Dickens (in terms of their broad public popularity - see, for example, the opening lines of Bleak House) must surely bear testament to rising public awareness.

> "Implacable November weather. As much mud in the streets as if the waters had but newly retired from the face of the Earth, and it would not be wonderful to meet a *Megalosaurus*, forty feet long or so, waddling like an elephantine lizard up Holborn Hill." Charles Dickens *Bleak House* (1853).

Owen's remarkable "elephantine lizards" were however to be short-lived in the public imagination. By the late 1850s new discoveries of more complete dinosaurs were to be made in the New World that were to transform the public perception of dinosaurs very significantly, though in truth the real story has some unexpected twists. In 1858 a partial skeleton of a dinosaur similar to Iguanodon was discovered in New Jersey. The animal, later named *Hadrosaurus* by Joseph Leidy of the Philadelphia Academy of Natural Sciences, had both front and back legs more or less intact, and it was suggested, because the front legs were so much shorter than the back ones, that the animal moved with an upright, or more kangaroo-like posture. Dramatic new restorations were made for science fairs in the US by Benjamin Waterhouse Hawkins, who had emigrated to take on projects of a similar nature to the one he had supervised at the Crystal Palace. Not only were the American dinosaurs different from Owen's version of British types, but in the following years the American Mid-West would yield some spectacular skeletons of dinosaurs. During the 1870s, 80s and 90s the world was treated to the most dramatic of feuds between two intelligent and resourceful men: Edward Drinker Cope of Philadelphia and Othniel Charles Marsh of Yale. This period, known colloquially as the time of the "Bone Wars" (Colbert, 1968; Desmond, 1975) though marked by considerable bitterness and animosity on the part of the two protagonists, resulted in the discovery of dozens of new and well-preserved dinosaurs - some preserved as fully articulated skeletons.

During this period of time the real diversity of dinosaurian anatomy began to emerge. It was appreciated that some dinosaurs had distinctly bird-like traits (particularly in the structure of their hips, legs and feet) while others were decidedly massive (such as *Brontosaurus* - the evocatively named "thunder-lizard" described by O.C. Marsh). On the basis of some of some of these differences Harry Govier Seeley (King's College London) identified two distinctive evolutionary lineages of dinosaurs that pass down to us today: **ornithischians** (bird-hipped forms) and **saurischians** (those with a more conventionally reptilian arrangement of bones). As a matter of pedantry, and the source of some obvious confusion, the bird-hipped forms are the group that are **not** closely related to birds.

Following this extremely exciting period of time (ending in the early decades of the twentieth century) the study of, and interest in, dinosaurs waned significantly. New discoveries continued to be made and reported, but for the most part these were workmanlike accounts and certainly not spiced by the rivalry that had marked previous decades. In the 1920s Mongolia proved to be a rich hunting ground for dinosaurs, yielding some bizarre forms, and also the first direct evidence of eggs and nests for dinosaurs. But it was not until later in this century that interest in the subject, and the role of dinosaurs in the larger history of life began to increase significantly in interest. Most importantly it was Professor John Ostrom who increased our interest in dinosaur biology and the relationship between dinosaurs and birds. Firstly he discovered a completely new type of dinosaur on an expedition to Montana. He called this creature *Deinonychus* and showed quite clearly that this was a truly amazing fast-moving, agile and highly intelligent killing machine; this shattered forever the image of dinosaurs as dull, plodding creatures shuffling toward their inevitable extinction at the end of the Cretaceous Period. It also ushered in a very new way of looking at dinosaurs - not merely as highly active, possibly endothermic, animals (which itself spawned a great deal of speculative "arm-waving") - but in the case of *Deinonychus*, animals that showed a surprising number of anatomical affinities with living birds. As a direct result of these two lines of investigation the level of activity and profile of dinosaurs has risen quite dramatically, culminating in recent years in very high-profile public interest resulting from the blockbuster film Jurassic Park. Despite the ridiculous plot and storyline for the film, what was remarkable was the portrayal of computer-designed and animated dinosaurs in an astonishingly realistic way. I still vividly remember, as a distinctly sceptical palaeontologist, my genuine amazement when I saw the "brachiosaur" feeding on a tree in the film. Jurassic Park not only dramatically increased public interest in dinosaurs (probably on a scale similar to the effect created by Owen's Crystal Palace dinosaur models) and their study, but also created a totally false impression of the work done by palaeontologists. So, despite the generalities hinted at above, the questions remain: what progress has been made during the 160 or so years since dinosaurs were first christened? and, is there a future for the study of the past?

The "Ages" of dinosaur research

Charting scientific progress in a field of research is an extremely inexact (I might be tempted to say futile) endeavour. In the case of dinosaur research one might choose to base estimations on the number of scientific papers produced per calendar year, the rate at which dinosaur names were added to the roster or the number of identifiable research workers active during defined periods of time - the list is entirely elastic, and justifications or caveats for exemption are equally many and various. In this instance I will attempt to chart a more epistemological route through the subject area, identifying, where I can, approaches and shifts in emphasis that have either an intellectual or in some instances technological origin.

Cuvierian comparative anatomy. Understanding the appearance and probable kinship of fossil animals, based on very fragmentary fossil remains, became possible in a more rigorous or systematic way through the painstaking work of Georges Cuvier in Paris. By publishing what were in effect libraries of the anatomy of living forms of animal Cuvier was able to demonstrate a uniformity to the way in which certain animals assemble the building blocks of their skeletons: birds are distinct from mammals, reptiles from fish, and at a more refined level wading birds could be distinguished anatomically from raptors. Using these principles he was able to compare isolated fossil bones to those found in living animals and in many instances reconstruct prehistoric animals with surprising (what must have seemed at the time almost magical) accuracy. Cuvier was also able to prove, quite conclusively, that animals (now wholly extinct) had lived at earlier times in Earth history - and that some were indeed bizarre and different from anything living today (Cuvier, 1812). This revelation had a galvanising influence on interest on the structure and fossil contents of the Earth.

So influential and dominant was Cuvier that all the early discoveries of dinosaurs were either sent (Gideon Mantell) or shown to him (William Buckland) directly and it is remarkable how perceptive his comments were. Cuvier recognised how distinct these remains were, and that they seemed to indicate extinct reptiles of elephantine proportions (Buckland, 1824) - foreshadowing in the 1820s what Owen would establish some twenty years later. The one weakness with Cuvier's approach was that it was unable to predict accurately the form of animals for which he did not have a modern analogue (such as dinosaurs). However Cuvier's influence persisted right through the last century, and still plays an important role in research today -we still use the principles of comparative anatomy to try to elucidate the form and relationships of newly discovered dinosaurs - as was the case during the discovery and study of the new English dinosaur *Baryonyx* during the 1980s and 90s.

The post-Darwinian period. The controversy generated by Charles Darwin's (1859) identification of Natural Selection as a mechanism by which change in morphology or behaviour can result in diversity among living animals had its impact on dinosaur research. This included the identification of anatomical links (presumed to be evolutionary) between, for example, modern birds and extinct dinosaurs as long ago as the late 1860s (Huxley, 1868). This followed the timely discovery of the "missing link" *Archaeopteryx* (Owen, 1863) in the Jurassic limestones of Bavaria, and the small, contemporary, predatory (and quite bird-like) dinosaur *Compsognathus*. Unfortunately there was no unanimity of opinion over the value of Natural Selection, and Darwin was reluctant to use evidence from a fossil record which seemed to him to be extremely patchy and therefore unreliable. So, during the post-Darwinian period much effort was placed firstly on simply adding more information to the fossil record - the prodigious labours of Marsh and Cope fall into this category of work - by adding the names and appearance and times of occurrence of more and more new species to the roster of the Dinosauria.

During this period some effort was made to try to gain a more complete understanding of the nature of these animals - Seeley, Huxley, Marsh and Cope were keen to chart a scheme by which dinosaurs might be classified consistently into an hierarchical (and by implication evolutionary) scheme. Also Louis Dollo (a less well known, French-born researcher who spent much of his life working in Belgium on a remarkable collection of dinosaur skeletons discovered at a coal-mine) began to apply biological methods to his analysis of fossil anatomy in order to try to establish the life-styles and behaviours of dinosaurs. He started by attempting to reconstruct their soft anatomy and used this to deduce, posture, locomotion, feeding habits and ultimately dinosaurian ecological roles in prehistoric ecosystems. Dollo was in many respects a precociously modern palaeobiologist but history has paid him little attention - though his name might be remembered in the form of "Dollos Law" - the principle of the irreversibility of evolution (once an organ/anatomical structure/ has been lost, it cannot be re-evolved in exactly the same form).

Dollo died in the early 1930s and was succeeded by various eminent workers who were less inclined to spend all of their time considering the detailed anatomy, biology or systematics of dinosaurian reptiles (Lull, Osborn, Romer, Simpson). Dinosaurs were increasingly perceived as a perhaps interesting, but nevertheless temporary, 'blip' in the much larger history of life. The very fact of their extinction 65 million years ago tended to reinforce the notion that they were irrelevant to strictly modern evolutionary or biological concerns and they increasingly became a matter of museological and curatorial concern, rather than the focus for primary research with the perhaps notable exceptions of Charles Gilmore (Smithsonian) and Friedrich von Huene (Tubingen).

The age of *Deinonychus*. Perhaps this is too much of a burden to place on one animal; it should rightly be credited to Professor John Ostrom (Yale) but, for reasons of euphony I have avoided the awkward "Ostromian". In the mid-l960s a new dinosaur Deinonychus ushered in a period of considerable activity and research on dinosaurs in a surprisingly wide range of biological and geological disciplines through the work of John Ostrom. *Deinonychus* single-handedly, or I should more accurately say "single-footedly," demolished decades of preconceptions concerning dinosaurs that dated back to the 1890s. This small, clearly lightly built, intelligent, highly active creature with many bird-like attributes at once called into question the notion that dinosaurs were slow moving, "cold-blooded", stupid or (most corrosively) evolutionary dead-beats. From the mid-1960s onward there was considerable controversy about the physiology of dinosaurs, which had an impact on the work of modern reptile and mammal physiologists; considerably more mainline research was done on old and new dinosaur discoveries completely revising, or revolutionising, many of the established notions about the posture, activity, mode of life interactions and relationships; dinosaur origins and extinctions became matters of crucial debate, and had an interaction at a sociological and environmentalist level with serious discussions pertaining to the perceived dangers of a "nuclear holocaust" and global disturbance to climates and environments paralleling what might have caused the extinction of dinosaurs (among other animals).

Modern dinosaur research programmes are remarkable in their range and variety, from basic descriptive anatomy in the case of new discoveries, through palaeobiological reconstructions, locomotor and postural studies, ecological studies, palaeophysiological analyses, taphonomic investigations, ecosystem analysis, trend analysis over geological times, palaeobiogeographical studies and their interactions with patterns and processes in evolutionary biology, ontogenetic evaluation (from growth series), pure systematic studies, and mechanical testing of virtual skeletons and CT-scanned reconstructions and analyses in three-dimensions. The range and variety of this type of work requires multidisciplinary skills, and is a sign of the remarkable vitality as I will demonstrate in the science of LONG DEAD THINGS.

References

Buckland, W. (1824). Notice on the Megalosaurus or great fossil lizard of Stonesfield. *Transactions of the Geological Society of London. 1* (2nd series) : 390-396.

Colbert, E. H. (1968). *Men and Dinosaurs. The search in field and laboratory*. London, Evans Brothers.

Cuvier, G. (1812). *Reserchès sur les ossemens fossiles de quadrupédes, où l'on rètablit les caractères de plusieurs espèces d'animaux que les révolution du globe paroissent avoir détruites*. Paris.

Darwin, C. R. (1859). *On the Origin of Species by means of Natural Selection; or the preservation of favoured races in the struggle for life*. London, John Murray.

Desmond, A. J. (1975). *The hot-blooded dinosaurs. A revolution in palaeontology*. London, Blond & Briggs.

Huxley, T. H. (1868). On the animals which are most nearly intermediate between birds and reptiles. *Annals of the Magazine of Natural History.* 2: 66-75.

ILN (1853). The Crystal Palace at Sydenham. *The Illustrated London News*. London. 23: 599-600.

ILN (1854). The Crystal Palace at Sydenham. *The Illustrated London News*. London. 24: 22.

McCarthy, S. and M. Gilbert (1994). The Crystal Palace Dinosaurs: the story of the world's first prehistoric sculptures. London, The Crystal Palace Foundation. Owen, R. (1842). Report on British Fossil Reptiles. Part 2. *Report of the British Association for the Advancement of Science (Plymouth). XI* (1841): 60-204.

Owen, R. (1854). *Geology and the Inhabitants of the Ancient World. (A guide-book to the Extinct Animals in the grounds of Crystal Palace)*. London, Crystal Palace Company.

Owen, R. (1863). On the Archaeopteryx of Von Meyer, with a description of the fossil remains of a long-tailed species, for the Lithographic Stone of Solenhofen. *Philosophical Transactions of the Royal Society of London*. 1863 : 33-47.

Torrens, H. S. (1992). When did the dinosaur get its name? *New Scientist. 134* (4 April 1992): 40-44.

Sponsors, Supporting Groups and Agencies

Amerada Hess
American Express
BBC
Blackwell Science
Blue Circle Industries
Burhouse
Brighton and Hove Council
Brighton and Hove GS
British Gas International
British Geological Survey
British Micromount Society
Cambrian Consultants
Chevron UK
Dinosaur Society
English Nature
Enterprise Oil
ESTA
Farnham Geological Society
FLAGS
Gemmological Society
GEOU
Harrow & Hillingdon Geological Society
IHS Energy
Institute of Petroleum
JAPEC
LandRover
ON Communications
Open University Geological Society
Nimr Petroleum
Nirex
Pavilion Internet
PESGB
PDP
Ravensbourne Geological Society
RJB Mining

Rockwatch
Royal Botanic Gardens Kew
RSNC
SEED
Shanks Waste Solutions
Southern Water
Sussex Mineral & Lapidary Society
The Clothing Company
The Coal Authority
The Hanson Environmental Fund
The Natural History Museum
The Russell Society
Tarmac
Time Computers
Travis Perkins
Virtual Logistics
Wandsworthians Memorial Trust
Yeoman